Scoop!

Noted journalist, author, diplomat and parliamentarian, Kuldip Nayar was born in Sialkot in 1924. He studied at Murray College in Sialkot and procured an LL.B from Law College in Lahore before joining the Medill School of Journalism in Northwestern University, Evanston. He served as press information officer to Gobind Ballabh Pant and Lal Bahadur Shastri, as high commissioner to the UK, and as a member of the Rajya Sabha, besides holding important positions in several news agencies and newspaper offices like UNI, PIB, the *Statesman* and the *Indian Express*. He was a correspondent of *The Times*, London, for twenty-five years. His syndicated column appears in over eighty publications around the world and he is the author of several books including *Between the Lines, Distant Neighbours: A Tale of the Subcontinent, India after Nehru* and *India House*.

Scoop!

INSIDE STORIES FROM THE PARTITION TO THE PRESENT

Kuldip Nayar

HarperCollins *Publishers* India
a joint venture with

New Delhi

HarperCollins *Publishers* India
a joint venture with
The India Today Group

Copyright © Kuldip Nayar 2006

Kuldip Nayar asserts the moral
right to be identified as the author of this work.

ISBN 13: 9788172236434
ISBN 10: 81-7223-643-3

First published in 2006
Third impression 2007

HarperCollins *Publishers*
1A Hamilton House, Connaught Place, New Delhi 110001, India
77-85 Fulham Palace Road, London W6 8JB, United Kingdom
Hazelton Lanes, 55 Avenue Road, Suite 2900, Toronto, Ontario M5R 3L2
and 1995 Markham Road, Scarborough, Ontario M1B 5M8, Canada
25 Ryde Road, Pymble, Sydney, NSW 2073, Australia
31 View Road, Glenfield, Auckland 10, New Zealand
10 East 53rd Street, New York NY 10022, USA

Typeset in 11.5/14.5 Bembo
Nikita Overseas Pvt. Ltd.

Printed and bound at
Thomson Press (India) Ltd.

To Raj, my sister,
and Rajinder Sachar, my brother-in-law,
who have always been there

Contents

Introduction

I DID NOT WANT TO BE A JOURNALIST. I HAD PASSED MY LL.B exam from Lahore and wanted to practice law in my hometown, Sialkot, but soon after I had taken the final examination, India was divided.

I travelled across the border from Sialkot to Amritsar, hoping to return when things settled down. But that never happened and so I came to Delhi in search of a job. I could have been a clerk, but that was not what I wanted. At the time, an Urdu newspaper owned by a Muslim businessman was looking for a Hindu journalist. I fulfilled the proprietor's requirements because he wanted his newspaper employee to also teach mathematics and English to his two children. The newspaper's name was *Anjam* (the end). In a way, I started my journalistic career from the end. I like to say, 'My *agaz* (beginning) was from *anjam*…'

At the newspaper, I was designated 'Joint Editor' because the proprietor's ulterior motive was to find a suitable person to help him appropriate the property of his brother who had migrated to Pakistan. He decided on my 'Joint Editor' designation in the hope that it would sound suitably impressive and open doors in the Ministry of Rehabilitation. (This was the ministry that decided on the allocation of properties left behind by those who migrated to Pakistan.)

My proprietor's tactics worked up to a point. My visiting card, with its important-sounding designation, did get me relevant access in the ministry. But, once inside, a senior official was frank enough to tell me that the property the owner was seeking had been designated 'enemy property' and could not be transferred.

When I passed on this information to him one day, the proprietor decided to terminate my services; he probably thought he would try and use someone else, to have another go at laying his hands on his brother's building.

Fortunately for me, another evening newspaper, *Wahadat*, in the same area of Billimaran, agreed to hire me for the same salary at Rs 100 a month. The work area comprised a large enclosed space, like a hall, in the corner of which a man lay on a cot, coughing endlessly. I asked one of my colleagues who the man was. He seemed surprised at my question because, so he thought, everyone knew the man on the cot was the poet and freedom fighter, Maulana Hasrat Mohani.

I was very fond of Mohani's poetry and in time he started to treat me as a member of his family. It was he who told me to resign from the newspaper and switch from Urdu to English because Urdu had no future in India.

Within a few days I had followed his advice and left for America. It was much easier in those days to get a visa and travelling by ship was inexpensive. I worked my way through – mowing lawns, washing windows and serving food. I returned home with an M.Sc. degree in journalism from Northwestern University in Evanston, near Chicago, and joined the Press Information Bureau, Government of India. The Jawaharlal Nehru Government had just initiated the First Five-Year Plan.

Subsequently, I became information officer of Home Minister Gobind Ballabh Pant and, after his death, of Lal Bahadur Shastri. During my days in the government, I was privy to some historic events, which I have narrated in this book. I particularly refer to the adoption of the Language Bill, which became necessary after the then home minister, Gulzarilal Nanda, wrongly issued a circular substituting Hindi for English as India's official language. This aroused the fears of non-Hindi-speaking people who had been assured by Jawaharlal Nehru that the switch-over would only take place with their approval.

I was in Tashkent when Prime Minister Shastri died. By that time, I had also started working unofficially for the UNI as its editor and general manager. From that time on, I spent the next two decades chasing news and breaking stories. Working as a journalist was very rewarding because of the sheer joy of ferreting out preciously guarded government secrets.

A part of the thrill was the feeling that you were doing a service to the country by functioning as a contemporary historian and recording significant developments for posterity. All that I have recounted here can be used as source material by researchers and others interested in covering those days. They may be scoops but they are also an insight into important events – how they happened and why.

In this book, for which I am grateful to Masooma Rafaqat Ali and Shyam Bhatia for their suggestions, I have interviewed practically all the presidents and prime ministers of India, Pakistan and Bangladesh. I have given insights into their thinking through some of the stories included in the book. But I will be discussing them in more detail when I publish my autobiography, *The Day Looks Old*.

Both, wittingly and unwittingly, I have interpreted the decisions of policy-makers to the public and the public's response to politicians and their officials. I may not have pleased many, but I have done my duty according to my conscience. People may differ with my viewpoint, but I can assure them that what I have expressed through my writings are my convictions and I have never feared nor favoured anybody.

In 1975, during the Emergency, Mrs Indira Gandhi detained me without trial because I wrote her a letter to point out that censorship was not consistent with democracy. (Her hardline response was a measure of the significant role that journalists could play in public affairs.)

It is sometimes said that a journalist's role is to inform, record, comment and sometimes entertain. All the above have been true for journalists of my generation, but at the time of Independence and afterwards, we were also cast in the exalted role of interpreting policy to the public and reporting the public's reaction back to the policy-makers. In part, this was because of the limited resources available to the mass media. In 1947, television had not been invented. The medium of communication was confined to radio and newspapers.

Those of us who analysed political developments soon became part and parcel of the national dialogue. Politicians sought us out so that we could relay their 'message' to a wider audience. Readers wanted to tell us what they thought about the men and women at the top. The combination added up to a golden age of political punditry that is now in the process of disappearing.

Why should this be? The answer lies in the new technology that has made it possible for the rulers to communicate directly with their subjects without the need of middlemen. Television, and to some extent the Internet, have made it possible to communicate directly with the masses. The man on the street no longer needs his or her political correspondent to tell him what the rulers are up to. People can make up their own minds by watching television. As for printed analyses, that is no longer the privilege of a few elite correspondents. The Internet has created space for bloggers who create their own websites full of information, interpretation and analyses. Sometimes bloggers are better informed than the editors of mainstream newspapers.

This does not mean that the role of the newspaper profession is over, only that the competition is much stronger. The ultimate winners can be from print, television, radio or the Internet. But the crown still goes to those who get the scoops.

Kuldip Nayar
August, 2006

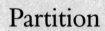

Partition

1

30 January, 1948

I WAS ONLY THREE-MONTHS-OLD IN *ANJAM*, AN URDU DAÌLY appearing from Billimaran in Old Delhi; which was also the span of my career in journalism. It was the only job which I could land quickly. Although I had a law degree from Lahore my forté was a degree in Persian and the knowledge of Urdu. I was then twenty-two.

Thrilled to be made a reporter-cum-subeditor without any experience, I would hang around the news agency ticker in the office and marvel at how quickly and relentlessly it belched out words. The afternoon of 30 January was one such occasion. I was near the ticker. A bell rang – it was a newsflash. This was the device used in those days to draw the attention of the news desk to any unexpected and important story.

'*Gandhi Shot!*' were the words that caught my eye. I felt as if my heart had stopped beating. The whole world seemed to collapse around me. What would we do without him? A colleague had a motorbike. He said he would drop me to Birla House where Mahatma Gandhi lived. It was the biggest story of my fledgling career and I knew I was not equipped for it. I had failed in the journalism course at Lahore; as I had in Urdu, an optional subject in the Bachelor of Arts (BA) degree course.

Gandhi could not die. He was all that we had, to check the chaos Partition had left in its wake. I was praying fervently as the motorbike sped towards Birla House. I recalled Gandhi's words, saying that he would die after winning Independence.

Sitting on the pillion of the motorbike, many things came before my eyes: saying goodbye to my parents in my hometown Sialkot, joining a caravan of people trudging towards India, and crossing the border with just Rs 120 in my pocket.

There was no unusual activity on the streets. Daryaganj, which divided old Delhi from New Delhi, was crowded as always. Further up, traffic was thin. The roads beyond India Gate were practically deserted – as they always were at the time. The wooden entrance gate to Birla House was shut but I managed to enter after showing them an identity card from my paper. I did not like the look of the place. It was desolate. Something pierced through me when I heard the chant 'Gandhi Amar Rahe' (Long Live Gandhi) – an invocation after the death of a great man.

Swathed in white khadi, a group of men and women stood around Gandhiji's body, drowned in their grief; others sat reading the Gita, the book Gandhiji loved. Many, who had come for the afternoon prarthana (prayer), which could not take place, had stayed behind, just to be around. Gandhiji used to hold the prayer on the platform at the end of Birla House, beginning with recitations from the Gita, followed by readings from the Koran and the Bible.

That day, a person from the same prayer crowd had killed him. He had paraded as a devotee; he had touched Gandhiji's feet and then he had shot him thrice, from close range. Gandhiji had been on his way to the platform on which he sat to lead the prayer. The drops of blood on the path were still fresh. Strewn on either side of the path were flowers which had been crushed in the melée that followed the arrest of the killer. I could spot Prime Minister Jawaharlal Nehru,

Home Minister Sardar Patel, Education Minister Abul Kalam Azad and Defence Minister Baldev Singh in the small crowd. They all looked lost and lonely; as if there was no one to guide them any more. Governor-General Mountbatten arrived soon after me. He saluted the body of the Mahatma, which was placed, by this time, on a dais.

'Thank God, the killer was not a Punjabi,' Baldev Singh told Mountbatten. 'He was not a Muslim either and we are broadcasting these facts because there is already tension in many cities.' Speaking of Gandhiji, Mountbatten once said that he was like Jesus Christ or Gautam Buddha. He had sensed this whenever he interacted with him, during the tumultuous days of the transfer of power.

By now people had started pouring into Birla House. The police was present in large numbers and had barricaded the area. Gandhiji would not have approved of this because he was against making a fuss over security. Leaders should not shun people, he used to say. The government had offered him security but he had refused it.

Birla House was a sea of humanity. All the people were singing Gandhi's favourite bhajan: '*Ishwar, Allah tere naam*', or raising the slogan: '*Gandhi Amar Rahe*'. Nehru climbed onto a boundary wall, and wiping his tears, said: 'The light has gone out of our lives. Bapu is no more. A glory has departed and the sun that warmed and brightened our lives has set and we are left to shiver in the cold and dark.' Nehru broke down while he spoke. So did the crowd. There was hardly a face without tears. Everyone felt as if they had lost a revered family elder, leaving the children orphaned and forlorn.

I did not see Nathuram Godse, the killer. He was locked into a room in Birla House itself. Only a few days earlier, the press had quoted Gandhi in conversation with BC Roy, the then West Bengal chief minister: 'What's the good of my living?' Gandhiji had said. 'Neither the people nor those in power have any use for me. "Do or Die" (the slogan he raised when he began the Quit India Movement on 9 August, 1942) becomes me more in the circumstances. I wish to die in harness, taking the name of God with my last breath.'

His wish was granted because when he fell, from the bullet shots in his chest, he said: 'Hé Ram, Hé Ram.' These very words were engraved on Gandhi's samadhi at Rajghat, the place, between Old and New Delhi, that Nehru chose as a memorial site for Gandhi.

During the Hindu–Muslim riots in Calcutta he had been a one-man force. Alone, he made the Hindus and the Sikhs surrender all their arms big and small, lethal and non-lethal which they had used to retaliate to the Muslim Direct Action petition. Who would quench the fire that Partition had ignited and the one which the Hindu Mahasabha and the Muslim League were trying to spread?

I took off my shoes and walked on the ground where Gandhiji used to hold the afternoon prayer. Something captured me. I think it was the air of asceticism or spiritualism which I thought I was inhaling. I recalled how, only a few days earlier, I had been part of the audience at the Mahatma's prayer meeting. It was the day that Madan Lal Pahwa had exploded a bomb behind the platform where Gandhi was sitting to deliver his speech. I had heard the noise but had not considered it anything more than a cracker because Gandhi had not reacted to the explosion. He had continued with his discourse as if nothing had happened. I only came to know from the morning newspapers the next day that it had been a bomb.

I recalled Gandhiji's words at that discourse: 'Hindus and Muslims are my two eyes.' Would the nation still heed the voice which a fanatic Hindu had silenced? Would his mission to foster pluralism be completed after his sacrifice? At least, in death, he had merged the different religious communities – Hindus, Muslims, Sikhs and Christians – into one multitude of sorrow. All of them mourned collectively for the loss of

Bapu. Still, conspirators, terrorists and fanatics came from nowhere to destroy the pluralistic society Gandhiji had tried to build. The fire of communal frenzy raged unabated. What it put out was, ironically, Gandhi's life. After his assassination everything froze in its tracks – crime as well as callousness. A shocked nation groped to find the light, which only Gandhiji had provided. There was also a feeling of guilt; the realization that their hatred had blinded the people of India and that one from among them had killed the greatest man on earth.

The newsroom in the office was engulfed in gloom when I returned. I did not talk to anybody. Like them, I felt insecure. We were afraid of tomorrow, of the future. None disturbed me as I sank into my chair to write my story. I had so much to say but I could not even hold my hands steady, let alone putting my fingers together to hold the pen. Some of the words I wrote were not legible because my tears smudged them. The editor called me and asked me to read out slowly what I had written. I broke down. It took me some time to gather myself and file my report.

My story ran thus:

The man called Mahatma Gandhi is no more. A Hindu fanatic, Nathuram Godse, killed him. But he has done something more. He has tried to revive madness in the name of religion.

Godse was not alone. The government believed that behind him was a conspiracy to undo the secular ethos of India. The Hindu Mahasabha was reportedly behind Godse. Around four in the evening, Gandhiji walked from his room, a little later than usual, to his prayer ground. Almost halfway, Godse shot him thrice as Gandhi fell uttering 'Hé Ram'.

I could not write further. The agency copy was added to mine. I was so overwhelmed with grief and anger that I did not translate the other report which the editor had given me. It was a news item about the communal riot that had broken out in Pune, the city from which Godse hailed. I was so upset that I did not want to hear, read or write anything about the riots. Gandhiji was a victim of a Hindu–Muslim riot. Why should I tell readers about yet another communal riot? The paper missed the story.

The editor called me the following morning, not to admonish me but to tell me that objectivity was one of the cardinal principles of journalism. I had to report the happenings as they unfolded, good or bad, without letting my feelings cloud my judgement. I realized that the editor was right.

Gandhiji's assassination made up my mind. I decided to stay in journalism. This was the profession through which Gandhiji's values could be disseminated. I have reported many communal riots since. But I have often wondered how long it will take India to let Gandhi's words – 'Hindus and Muslims are my two eyes' – come true? When will the two communities begin to follow his path and spread the message he had tried to instil? After all, wrong methods cannot lead to the right results.

2

A Chance Encounter with Jinnah

I WAS IN MY SECOND YEAR AT LAW COLLEGE IN LAHORE WHEN the Qaid-e-Azam, the title given by Mahatma Gandhi to Mohammed Ali Jinnah, came visiting to our college. This was some time in 1945. Although Lahore was where the Pakistan resolution had been adopted, Jinnah had generally avoided the city. He had not been able to win over either Punjab or the areas beyond the North-west Frontier Province, Baluchistan and Sind, the area which constituted West Pakistan and ultimately Pakistan. Khan Abdul Ghaffar Khan, popularly known as the Frontier Gandhi, dominated the Frontier province and Khan Abdus Samad Khan, known as Baluchi Gandhi, prevailed over Baluchistan. Punjab itself was under the Unionist government, headed by Khizar Hayat Khan Tiwana. However, Jinnah's Muslim League was making inroads in these parts, although its main strength was in UP, Bihar and Bengal.

The turn-out for Jinnah's lecture was poor. Habib, my classmate, had first kept out all non-Muslims. But when he found only a slim crowd in attendance he personally requested the Hindu and Sikh students to attend the lecture. Still, the venue of the lecture had to be changed from the auditorium to a classroom. The point to note was that the provinces that constituted Pakistan had not much support for the idea of a separate Muslim nation even two years before the country was divided on the basis of religion.

Jinnah looked elegant in his three-piece suit, and did not seem to mind the poor attendance. He spoke about his dream of Pakistan like an evangelist. You could oppose him or support him but you could not ignore him. He and Pakistan were a reality. He said something to the effect that it was important to understand that a united India would not give Muslims a feeling of independence because the Hindus would be in a majority. A non-Muslim nation would be ruling the Muslim nation. But, both nations, if made independent in their separate countries, would grow according to their own genius. Both would contribute towards each other's development.

After the lecture, which lasted for half an hour, Jinnah said he would welcome questions from the floor. I put him two questions, which seem prophetic in hindsight.

The first question expressed my fears. I asked him whether, given the way in which hatred and enmity between Hindus and Muslims had been sown and strengthened in the last few years, it would be natural for the two communities to jump at each other's throat after the British left.

Jinnah did not share my fears. Nor did he expect communal riots. With his monocle held daintily between his fingers, Jinnah replied that there was nothing that linked the two nations. But if they were to separate they would live happily; there would not be any conflict. 'Blood is thicker than water' was his assurance. He said that the estrangement I found between the two nations would disappear the day the nations became independent. Pakistan and India would live as good neighbours. 'Some nations have killed millions of each other's people and yet, an enemy of today is a friend of tomorrow,' he said.

Years later, when I went to Pakistan to collect material for my book, *Distant Neighbours- A Tale of the Subcontinent* in early 1971, I enquired from K.H. Khurshid, Jinnah's secretary, how Jinnah had reacted to the rioting, especially to the population migration. Both the Muslim League and the Congress had termed it 'preposterous' when it was formally proposed to them.

Khurshid replied that the Qaid-e-Azam would not at first believe that there was any large-scale rioting. Later, he maintained that 'they wanted to undo Pakistan'. His reference was to the Congress and the Akalis, not the British. Eventually, Khurshid told me, the Qaid-e-Azam was glum and withdrawn.

Khurshid and I analysed the cause of rioting. He alleged that the Hindu Mahasabha, the Akalis and 'some communal elements in the Congress' ignited the riots. I said that he was probably right, but the Muslim League was no less responsible. I specifically recalled the Direct Action call given by the then Bengal chief minister S. Suhrawardy in 1946. When asked whether Direct Action would be violent or nonviolent, Jinnah had said: 'I am not going to discuss ethics.'

The Direct Action resulted in the 'Great Calcutta Killing'. Over 5000 people lost their lives in less than three days. Khurshid defended Jinnah, arguing that the Qaid-e-Azam was in favour of a pluralistic Pakistan. He drew my attention again and again to Jinnah's speech in the Pakistan Constituent Assembly: 'You are free to go to your temples. You are free to go to your mosques or to any other place of worship in this state of Pakistan. You may belong to any religion or caste or creed; that has nothing to do with the business of the state. You will find that in the course of time, Hindus will cease to be Hindus and Muslims will cease to be Muslims, not in the religious sense, because that is the personal faith of each individual, but in the political sense as citizens of the state.'

I told Khurshid that it was because of this speech of Jinnah's that we did not leave our home in Sialkot city till 13 September, one month after Partition.

My second question to Jinnah was: What would Pakistan's response be if a third country attacked India?

He replied, without any hesitation, that Pakistan would stand by India. Our soldiers, he said, would fight by your side to defeat the enemy.

Such a situation arose when China attacked India in 1962. Mohammed Ayub Khan was then Pakistan's chief martial law administrator. Within Pakistan there were demands that it should take advantage of India's adversity. Zulfikar Ali Bhutto told me that if Pakistan had attacked India at that time, 'we could have gone up to Delhi'. Ayub explained to me that the reason why he did not act at that time was that he did not want to embarrass India. When I said that he did not do so probably at the bidding of America and Britain, he said: 'No, I assure you… I did not want to stab India in the back, although I sometimes wonder whether I did the right thing.'

After the attack, Jawaharlal Nehru wrote to all countries, including Pakistan, to explain how the Chinese had attacked India to enforce their territorial claims by military might. Ayub replied tersely: 'I agree with you when you say that no effort should be spared to eliminate deceit and force from international relations. In this respect, I am constrained to point out that various outstanding disputes between India and Pakistan can also be resolved amicably should the government of India decide to apply these principles with sincerity and conviction.'

Ayub's reply disappointed Nehru but one phrase which pleased him was that the Sino–India conflict was 'endangering the peace and stability of the region in which Pakistan is vitally concerned'. India was able to pull away some of its troops from the Pakistan border for deployment against China.

3

Mountbatten's Role in Partition

I WROTE TO LORD LOUIS MOUNTBATTEN, THE LAST BRITISH governor-general of India, in late July 1971, asking for an interview to discuss his part in the Partition of the country. He did not respond. So, when I reached London, towards the end of September, I rang him up. After great reluctance, he agreed to meet me. He was then living at Broadlands, a sprawling mansion, not far from London, and he sent his grandson to the railway station to receive me.

For late September, it was a cool, clear day. Mountbatten sat in a cane chair on a neatly mowed lawn, partially hidden by the long shadows cast by the receding sun. He knew I was resident editor of the *Statesman* in New Delhi.

After settling down, the first question I asked Mountbatten was: 'Do you regret the Partition?'

'I do, but I had no choice. When I went in it was too late. Had I gone to India when Lord Archibald Wavell (his predecessor) did, I might have succeeded in keeping the country together,' he replied.

Soon he was talking about Partition as if he had wanted to talk about it for a long time but had had no opportunity to do so. His memory did not fail him even once as he narrated events that went as far back as 1947. The annoying part was his self-righteousness – as if he had made no mistakes while the others had. It was irritating to hear him refer to Pandit Jawaharlal Nehru as 'my prime minister' and Sardar Vallabhbhai Patel as 'my home minister'. If at all he was respectful, it was to Mahatma Gandhi: 'Whenever he came in, I felt that some celestial light had entered my room,' recalled Mountbatten. He mentioned Mohammed Ali Jinnah, the founder of Pakistan, with scant respect.

Although he took me to the room where his papers and records were stacked neatly on the almirah shelves and file-racks, Mountbatten did not accede to my request to see them. 'The papers are the property of a trust, named after me, and it will decide what to do with them.'

Mountbatten made no secret that Lord Clement Attlee, the then British prime minister, wanted to keep India united. 'Before departing for Delhi his advice to me was to think of some arrangement, a loose federation or a central mechanism, to maintain contact between the two.' But other British leaders told him when he left London that there was no way out except Partition. 'I tried to preserve unity but Jinnah did not agree,' Mountbatten assured Attlee. He claimed that he had argued in favour of one India but Jinnah's reply had been that, even though nothing would have given him greater pleasure than to see such unity, it was the behaviour of the Hindus that had made it impossible for the Muslims to accept.

Whether the 'behaviour of the Hindus' was to blame or not, one thing certain was that the Muslims, at the time, were extremely perturbed about their future. They had little fear in the areas where they were in a majority but, being in a minority in India as a whole, they were plagued by the thought that their position and status in independent India would not be secure. Maulana Abul Kalam Azad, a top Congress leader, had warned Muslims that after India's division they would discover that they had become aliens and foreigners in their own country. Backward industrially, educationally and economically, they would be left to the mercy of what would then become an unadulterated Hindu Raj.

Alan Campbell-Johnson, Mountbatten's press attaché, recalled how Jinnah, during a dinner at the viceroy's house, was so worried about Pakistan eluding him that he said: 'The Congress will accept even dominion status to deprive me of Pakistan.'

'Do you know that you are held responsible for the one million people killed during Partition?' I asked Mountbatten. 'The change of the date of British departure, from 6 June 1948 to 15 August 1947, heightened tension on both sides and led to the forced transfer of populations and the massacre.'

Mountbatten did not deny the sequence of events. He said: 'I could not hold the country together. I had to hasten the process.' He rationalized the killing thus: 'When I go before the Almighty I shall tell Him that when I was commanding the navy from Singapore during World War II, I saved the lives of 2½ million people by diverting food ships to Bengal despite Churchill's persistent refusal. I will plead with Him that my account is still 1½ million plus.'

London informed Mountbatten about the visit of three cabinet ministers: Fredrick William Pethick-Lawrence, then secretary of state for India, Sir Stafford Cripps and A.V. Alexander. On their arrival, they said that the British wanted the Indians to set up an 'acceptable' machinery to realize full independent status and to make interim arrangements in the meantime. They had brought along with them a formula which came to be known as the Cabinet Mission Plan.

The Plan divided the country into three zones: A, B and C. Zone A would embrace all Hindi-speaking states in the north and the Congress-ruled states in the south; Zone B would include Punjab, Sind, the NWFP and Baluchistan. Zone C included Bengal and Assam. The three ministries: defence, foreign affairs and communications would, however, belong compulsorily to the central government. Both the Congress and the Muslim League initially accepted the plan. However, Nehru, after becoming Congress president, said that, 'the party would enter the Constituent Assembly completely unfettered by agreement and free to treat all situations as they arise'.

Jinnah did not like Nehru's statement, which he thought was a trick to deny the Muslims autonomy. He reiterated the demand for Pakistan as the only course left open to the Muslim League and rescinded its earlier resolution to accept the Cabinet Mission Plan.

Nehru's objection was to the grouping of the states in zones. He wanted a state which was in a particular group to have the option of moving to another group. The Cabinet Mission Plan officially clarified that the grouping of states was an integral part of their proposal and could not be changed. Maulana Abul Azad went on record to say that Nehru was wrong and that the Congress could not modify the plan 'as it pleased'.

Why Nehru turned against the Mission Plan is difficult to say. It could be because of his experience with the Interim government earlier, when the Muslim League ministers did not cooperate with him. After the then finance minister Liaqat Ali Khan's order that all posts, including those of peons, would have to come to him for approval, things became hell for the Congress ministers. They felt so exasperated that they were even prepared to part ways.

'Once the Agreement on the Cabinet Mission Plan broke down,' Mountbatten said, 'I had no choice except to work on Partition.' He was not happy. He blamed the collapse of the Cabinet Mission Plan on the misunderstanding created by Nehru. But Partition was now inevitable. He was summoned to London for consultations. On his return, Mountbatten immediately began to work on a plan for Partition. Once the draft was ready, he consulted Nehru and Sardar Patel who accepted it readily; they were getting old and wanted to participate in building the new India of their dreams. Maulana Abul Kalam Azad once mentioned to me that this had made him feel left out. He had gone to Gandhi – who had earlier walked out of Mountbatten's room when he heard the word 'partition'—but Gandhi was no solace for Azad.

Mountbatten said that after getting the approval of Nehru and Patel, he called Jinnah and told him that his demand for Pakistan had become a reality. 'I asked Jinnah whether he would accept anything less or any tie with India, loose or firm,' Mountbatten said. 'Jinnah said no. "I do not trust them."'

Mountbatten once again went to London to work out the Partition plan. Disappointed, Attlee wondered if there was still some way to stop the vivisection of India. Winston Churchill, the British prime minister during World War II, told Mountbatten that India would have to be divided if the British were to quit.

Mountbatten recalled that the main discussion was on Bengal and Punjab. He insisted on partitioning the two provinces on the same principle as had been applied to the subcontinent while Jinnah insisted on keeping them wholly in Pakistan. When Mountbatten explained to him the logical consequences of Partition, that is, dividing Punjab and Bengal, it took Jinnah some time to grasp its reality. He had not realized it would happen that way and that soon. Mountbatten regretted that it was inevitable after his failure to sustain any ties between India and Pakistan.

Jinnah then argued that the people of Bengal and Punjab were first Bengalis and Punjabis and then Hindus and Muslims. 'How could I have accepted the logic? That applied to the whole of India,' said Mountbatten. And he therefore rejected the plea. What else could he have done when Jinnah himself had remained silent on a question posed by Gandhi in a letter dated 14 September 1944, asking whether Bengalis,

Tamilians or Maharashtrians would 'cease to have their special characteristics if all of them became converts to Islam?'

'I told Jinnah that his moth-eaten Pakistan will not last more than twenty-five years,' reminisced Mountbatten. 'You know, Rajaji (C. Rajagopalachari, the last Indian governor-general), wrote to me the other day to say that my prophecy had come true, and I replied that I remembered my words distinctly,' Mountbatten said again, to emphasize his point, lest he should be accused of seeing this only in hindsight.

(I checked both with H.V. Hudson, a British historian associated with the Partition plan, and Campbell-Johnson, whether Mountbatten had ever mentioned earlier that East Pakistan would break away from West Pakistan. They said they were hearing this for the first time.)

4

The Radcliffe Award

'I NEARLY GAVE YOU LAHORE,' JUSTICE LORD CYRIL RADCLIFFE, chairman of the Boundary Commission, told me. 'But, then I realized that Pakistan would not have any large city. I had already marked Calcutta to India.' Lahore had Hindus and Sikhs in a majority and was way up in assets. He sounded convincing, but really he had no other option because Pakistan had a paucity of large towns.

Radcliffe was formally dressed in a jacket and a necktie. He had been a judge for a long time and it was probably his habit to wear a jacket when he met a visitor. But there was no formality in his manner. I found him a simple, straightforward person during my conversation with him. He opened the door himself when I rang the bell of his flat. The room was cluttered with old furniture, with things he must have collected over the years. The living appeared austere. He had no servant or maid because he went himself to a kitchenette, which I could see from the sofa in the sitting room, to place a kettle on the burner to prepare tea.

This conversation took place in Radcliffe's flat in London towards the latter half of 1971, when I had gone there to meet Lord Mountbatten, the last British governor-general. I wanted to know how the boundary lines of India and Pakistan had been drawn. Although the Boundary Commission had four more members – two from India, Mehar Chand Mahajan and Teja Singh, and two from Pakistan, Din Mohammed and Mohammed Munir – they were all serving judges. Radcliffe was the one who had actually made the decision, because the Commission had been divided; India's members on one side and those from Pakistan on the other.

What yardstick did Radcliffe apply? I was keen to know. I found to my horror that Radcliffe had had no fixed rules to go by when he drew the boundaries between India and Pakistan. He had gathered sufficient data by the time he came to demarcate the borders. The two sides were exhaustive in their presentation. He had read tonnes of material as well. The ticklish part of his assignment, he said, was to partition the last track of Punjab and Bengal on the basis of religion. Therefore, his decision to give Lahore to India and then to reverse it in favour of Pakistan was understandable. He had some kind of balance in mind. That Mohammed Ali Jinnah, founder of Pakistan, had recommended Radcliffe's name, had nothing to do with it.

'Are you satisfied with the way you drew the border lines between India and Pakistan?' I asked.

'I had no alternative; the time at my disposal was so short that I could not do a better job. Given the same amount of time, I would do the same thing again. However, if I had two to three years, I might have improved on what I did,' admitted Radcliffe. He had just flown once over parts of northern India in a Dakota before demarcating the borders. 'If the aspirations of some people were not fulfilled,' he said, 'the fault lies in the political arrangements, with which I am not concerned.'

Indeed, Radcliffe was given very little time to finish his work. He was delayed because the provincial assemblies of Punjab and Bengal had to vote for the division of the two provinces, a legal obligation. Radcliffe was in Shimla when

Mountbatten nominated him the chairman of the Boundary Commission. He told me that he would have preferred to work in Punjab in July. 'It was impossible to undertake the field survey in June because of the heat,' he said. But Mountbatten, according to Maulana Abul Kalam Azad told Radcliffe that he could not delay the work even by a day. Mountbatten would telephone him at least twice a day!

Radcliffe was not happy with the members on the Boundary Commission. All that they did, he said, was to put across the point of view of the country they represented. Both sides wanted maximum territory and argued at cross-purposes. One Muslim member came to him in private and pleaded for Darjeeling's inclusion in Pakistan: 'My family goes to Darjeeling every summer and it would be hard on us if the place went to India.' Radcliffe had a good word for Mehar Chand Mahajan, the Indian Boundary Commission member who subsequently became India's chief justice. He impressed Radcliffe with his erudition and legal knowledge.

'The Muslims in Pakistan nurture the grievance that you favoured India,' I told Radcliffe. He replied that they should be grateful to him because he had gone out of his way to give them Lahore 'which deserved to go to India. Even otherwise, I favoured the Muslims more than the Hindus'.

It seemed that criticism of the boundaries he had delineated had reached his ears by the time I met him. He was irritated when I mentioned 'the unhappiness' of the Pakistanis. What hurt him most was the allegation that he had changed his report at Mountbatten's instance. The allegation of the Pakistanis was that Mountbatten had put pressure on Radcliffe to give India the Firozepur and Zira tehsils to provide a link with Jammu and Kashmir.

'I was not even aware of Kashmir,' Radcliffe said. 'I heard about it long after I returned to London.'

During the conversation, which lasted for more than one hour, I told him about the sharp differences between India and Pakistan over Kashmir. He was aware of them. He also knew about the wars the two countries had fought against each other. He felt sorry about what had happened. But he remained firm in his assertion that he gave Firozepur and Zira to India because that was what he believed was correct. He repeatedly told me that there was no pressure on him to do so. The only pressure exerted on him was to submit an early report, he said.

On 22 July, 1947, writing to Radcliffe, Mountbatten said that he had a discussion in Lahore with the Punjab Partition Committee.

Referring to the assurance he had given the Committee, promising that he would write to Radcliffe and emphasize the urgency of the earliest possible date for the Punjab Boundary Award, Mountbatten said: 'It was emphasized (in the Punjab Paritition Committee) that the risk of disorder would be greatly increased if the Award was to be announced at the very last moment before the 15th of August. I know that you fully appreciate this, but I promised that I would mention it again to you, and say that we would all be grateful for every extra day earlier that you could manage to get the Award announced. I wonder if there is any chance of getting it out by the 10th?'

Replying the next day, Radcliffe said: 'I will certainly bear in mind the importance of the earliest possible date for the Award ... I do not think that I could manage the 10th. But I think that I can promise the 12th, and I will do the earlier day, if I possibly can.'

I did not ask Radcliffe about the letter Mountbatten's naval attaché George Abell had written to Abott, secretary to the Punjab governor, since I was not aware of its existence at that time. The letter, dated 8 August 1947, said: 'I enclose a map showing roughly the boundary which Sir Cyril Radcliffe promised to demarcate in the Award and a note describing it. There will not be any great changes from this boundary, but it will have to be accurately defined with reference to the village and zilla boundaries of Lahore district.'

The Punjab governor, Roy Jenkins, wrote to Mountbatten: 'The enclosures were a schedule, I think, typed, and a section of a printed map with a line drawn thereon, together showing a boundary which included in Pakistan a sharp salient in the Firozepur district. This salient enclosed the whole of Firozepur and Zira tehsils.' Jenkins also stated that: 'About the 10th or 11th August when we were still expecting the Award on 13 August, at latest, I received a message from the Viceroy's house containing the words "eliminate salient"…The change caused some surprise, not because the Firozepur salient had been regarded as inevitable or even probable, but because it seemed odd that any advance information had been given by the Commission when the Award was not substantially complete.'

It was ironical that Radcliffe, who divided India into two independent countries, advised 'some joint control' when it came to splitting the irrigation network of the Punjab between India and Pakistan. His Award gave the irrigation canals to Pakistan and the rivers feeding them to India, while the controlling headworks were evenly divided. But he continued to hint at 'some joint control'. India's then prime minister Jawaharlal Nehru, rejected it and characterized it as 'a political recommendation'.

Since there was no 'joint control', the two countries, after the division, argued endlessly over their respective rights. Pakistan said that the rivers were common to the subcontinent and maintained that it was the sole owner of the waters and the headwork in its territory. It became such a divisive issue that Rawalpindi suggested that the matter be referred to the International Court of Justice at the Hague. But Nehru opposed the idea on the grounds that it would be 'a confession of our continued dependence on others'.

Before saying goodbye to Radcliffe I posed the same question which I had asked Mountbatten. Did Mohammed Ali Jinnah hesitate when Pakistan was conceded? Mountbatten had said that he hadn't. Radcliffe's reply was: 'It is very unlikely.'

I also checked with him the truth of Mountbatten's claim that he had warned Jinnah that 'his moth-eaten Pakistan will not last more than twenty-five years'. Radcliffe said, 'You are the first person to have told me this. I never heard it before.'

As I left his flat, I wondered how India and Pakistan came to sign the Indus Basin Treaty.

In 1951, when Pakistan had been on the point of referring the dispute to the Security Council, an article by David E. Lilienthal, former chairman of the US Tennessee Valley Authority, appearing in an American magazine, saved the situation. He suggested a comprehensive engineering plan under which India and Pakistan could develop the entire Indus Basin jointly, 'perhaps with the help of the World Bank'. Apparently, Lilienthal had consulted Eugene E. Block, the then World Bank chief, before writing the article. Both India and Pakistan saw to it that America too would give its blessings to the proposal. The development of the Indus Basin was found acceptable by India and Pakistan when the funds were promised. Since it suggested a way out, and was also laced with money, the Indus Basin Treaty was signed in 1960 between Nehru and General Ayub Khan, the martial law administrator.

In response to the formal proposal by the World Bank chief (November, 1951), a 'working team' of engineers had been appointed to tackle problems outside the political arena. India gave a guarantee not to disturb supplies until the end of the negotiations – and it kept its word though Pakistan continued to make allegations to the contrary. For nine years, the negotiations between India and Pakistan covered a long, tortuous route, and even in the last stages, both Nehru and

Ayub Khan had to intervene to put the talks back on the track when the prejudice and cussedness of officials looked like derailing them. Pakistan had no problem because it was under military rule.

Nehru had to face criticism in parliament for accepting 19 per cent of the Indus Basin waters and agreeing to continue deliveries till Pakistan built alternative channels. Indian engineers had prepared a formidable case to prove that both Punjab and Rajasthan would be practically ruined if India were to stay its hands for the ten-year transitional period. Morarji Desai, then a member of Nehru's Cabinet, organized opposition from political quarters. Even Gobind Ballabh Pant, the union home minister, who was loyal to Nehru, expressed his unhappiness over India's 'heavy contribution' to the Indus Basin Development Fund. He wanted to get it adjusted against the value of the property that Hindu refugees had left in Pakistan.

Nehru brushed aside all objections. He was anxious to build good relations with Rawalpindi and thought a settlement of the water dispute would serve as the foundation upon which he could raise a durable structure of Indo–Pakistan amity.

Why didn't it happen?

The successive rulers at New Delhi should give the answer.

5

The Fallout of Partition

A YOUNG NAVAL ATTACHÉ OF THE QAID-E-AZAM Mohammed Ali Jinnah was greatly perturbed by the avalanche-like migration after Partition. Humanity was on the move in both Pakistan and India. No one had expected it. No one wanted it. But none could help it. The two countries blamed each other. This did not stop the Muslims from coming to Pakistan and the Hindus from going to India. He was personally concerned because his own relatives were stuck somewhere. Why migration? Was it inevitable? And what about the killings? Hundreds of thousand were suffering. Who was to blame?

With these disturbed thoughts the young naval-attaché went, as usual, to lunch at the government house in Karachi where his boss, Jinnah, would eat with his staff. In the the course of the meal, he asked the Qaid-e-Azam: 'Sir, was Pakistan necessary? The suffering of the people was beyond imagination. How would the future take shape?' He muttered these words to the amazement of everyone around the table, including Fatima Jinnah. There was complete silence. Even otherwise, disturbances and migrations lay heavy on everybody's hearts. Everyone looked towards Jinnah who took some time to react.

Jinnah finally said he had no answer to the questions asked. Only posterity would give its verdict. 'We are too near the events to make any judgement.' Then he lapsed into silence and, after a while, got up and left the dining table.

Subsequently, when the rioting did not stop, Jinnah picked on the Sikhs, whom he had tried to wean away from India with the promise of an autonomous Sikkim-type state (Azad Punjab) on the border of Pakistan and India.

His secretary, Khurshid Ahmed, told me in Lahore many years later, that Jinnah had never visualized such large-scale massacres and migrations. His idea of Pakistan, Khurshid said, was that of a parliamentary democracy where there would be no difference between Muslims and non-Muslims. Strange thinking for a person who had preached the two-nation theory and wanted nothing less than a homeland for Muslims.

In India, Sardar Patel was anxious that all Hindus and Sikhs should leave West Pakistan; he reportedly cared little for the Muslims whom he thought had better all leave since they had achieved what they wanted – Pakistan.

With Jawaharlal Nehru, pluralism was a matter of faith; he would even go himself to the streets of New Delhi to personally chase away Hindus looting Muslim shops. But the refugees from both sides carried with them to the country they went, not only bitterness and vengeful thoughts but also stories of atrocities commited on them in the very place where they had lived peacefully with each other for centuries.

On paper, both India and Pakistan declared that 'there shall be no discrimination against those who may have been political opponents before 15 August'. In practice, there was no sense of accommodation, no sense of forgiveness. The two countries behaved as the Congress party and the Muslim League had done before Partition; it was the same old effort to put the other side down. And this was worse – murder, destruction and looting.

Whichever side was to blame – or, rather, more to blame – the few weeks of madness on both sides of the border embittered relations between the two countries for generations to come. The two countries would differ on every subject, at every step. Fear and mistrust of each other made even trivial matters major issues.

So wide was the hiatus at that time, that Mohammed Ali Jinnah thought of breaking off diplomatic relations with India. He confided to Lord Ismay, a British dignitary who visited him in Karachi in September 1947, that 'there is no alternative but to fight it out'. Jinnah genuinely believed that India wanted to destroy his country – a fear that torments Pakistan even today.

In fact, from the very day the two countries came into being, recriminations began piling up. Pakistan blamed India for not letting it establish itself. When the dislocation of train services, owing to riots, hampered the dispatch of government records from Delhi to Karachi, Pakistan saw in it an Indian plot to sabotage the new country's administration. (The delay must have helped Karachi because it was able to do away with so much red tape!) And when the Joint Defence Council was disbanded four months earlier (30 November, 1947) than scheduled, the Pakistan government's conclusion was that this was a device to deprive it of military stores.

But then it was true that New Delhi did not send all the equipment and stores generously pledged at one time. And even Field Marshal Claude Auchinleck, the commander-in-chief of the Pakistan army, accused India of having designs to 'prevent Pakistan receiving her just share or indeed anything of arsenals and depots in India', and described Pakistan's attitude as 'reasonable and cooperative'. By this time the Kashmir war was on and India could not have been expected to give arms at a time when Pakistan's regular and irregular troops were advancing towards Srinagar which had come under New Delhi's wing after signing the 'Instrument of Accession'.

Again, Kashmir came in the way of New Delhi transferring its share of the cash balances to Karachi of undivided India. The Arbitration Tribunal had fixed Pakistan's share at Rs 750 million. New Delhi paid only Rs 200 million and withheld the rest because, to quote, Patel, 'India cannot reasonably be asked to make payment of cash balances when an armed conflict with its (Pakistan's) forces is in progress.' Pakistan's reply was that at no stage of the negotiations was the Kashmir question 'ever mentioned or considered' and, therefore, linking the two was an 'unfriendly act'.

An important section in the Indian Government favoured the adjustment of Pakistan's share against the property left by Hindus and Sikhs in Pakistan. A rough estimate was that evacuee property in Pakistan totalled Rs 500 crores ($375 million) as against Rs 100 crores ($75 million) in India – a ratio of five to one. Agricultural land left in India was 4,800,000 acres and in Pakistan 3,139,000 acres.

It was only after the protest fast of Mahatma Gandhi – who was appalled by the damage which the non-payment of dues to Karachi was causing to Indo–Pakistan relations – that New Delhi paid Pakistan's share. Patel never forgave the Mahatma for this. Nor did the extremist Hindus, one of whom assassinated him on 30 January, 1948.

The two countries fell out over trade too. There was a deadlock on the earlier agreement to exempt goods shipped from India to Pakistan and vice-versa from customs duty. It was a sort of a Customs Union, but it did not work. Instead, both countries began treating each other as 'foreign' for purposes of levying customs and excise duties. The result was that India looked to Egypt for cotton which could have been available from across the border, and Pakistan hauled coal all the way from Britain and America instead of getting it from the nearby mines of Bihar.

Had there been any redeeming feature, any other bright patch in India–Pakistan relations, or had the people on both sides settled down to accept the reality of Partition, things might have been different. But the climate in the subcontinent was one of hate and revenge.

The Nehruvian Years

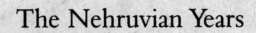

6

The Status of Hindi

HOME MINISTER GOBIND BALLABH PANT WAS, INDEED, UPSET.
His mentor, Prime Minister Jawaharlal Nehru, had not liked
the report which a Parliamentary Committee, headed by Pant,
had prepared, to recommend Hindi as the principal language
and English as a subsidiary one, with no target date for the
switch-over. The Indian Constitution had laid down 26
January 1965, as the deadline for the change-over from
English to Hindi.

Nehru, couched in the environment of the English
language, was furious to find the word 'subsidiary' being used
for English. He told Pant that it meant that English was the
language of 'vassals'. Pant sent me, his information officer, to
visit every library in Delhi to collect as many dictionaries as I
could. I found in some of them, that the word 'subsidiary'
had 'additional' as an alternative interpretation.

Pant wrote to Nehru that the two words, 'subsidiary' and
'additional', meant more or less the same thing. He quoted
from the Madras Government's Memorandum, submitted
to the centre, to point out how the word 'subsidiary' was
used for English even by a South Indian state which was all
for English. The memorandum said : 'It is possible, by 1965,

to promote Hindi to the status of principal official language of the union, if provision is made for continuing English as a subsidiary official language thereafter.'

Nehru did not accept Pant's argument. Instead, he expressed his anger on the phone. I could see that Pant was visibly hurt after the call. He could not get over the fact that, of all persons, Nehru, his hero, had ticked him off. Pant did not tell me what Nehru had advised but remarked: 'Hindi will never be India's lingua franca. You will see it. I shall be dead by that time. Panditji has made things difficult.' That very day Pant had his first heart attack.

Pant did not change the report and retained the word 'subsidiary'. He backed his preference for the word by sending Nehru various interpretations of 'subsidiary' in English. That day I ransacked every library in Delhi to collect as many dictionaries as possible. In some of them, 'subsidiary' had 'additional' as an alternate meaning. But the government's records showed that the words, 'additional' and 'associate', were used officially for English. The word 'subsidiary' was quietly dropped from the records.

I knew how much Pant had worked to have a unanimous report to give Hindi recognition as the principal language of India. I had attended the Parliamentary Committee's meetings and seen how uphill the task had been. I saw Pant moving at the Committee, step by step, slipping at times, but starting all over again, to reconcile the differences. MPs were divided into two groups: pro-Hindi and pro-English. Ultimately he won and brought around all the members of the Committee to one point of view.

The journey began in 1955 when the government constituted a Committee of 35 members from the Lok Sabha and the Rajya Sabha to consider the recommendations of the Official Language Commission. It was obligatory to appoint one under a provision by the Constitution to assess how far Hindi had progressed and whether it had spread enough in the past five years since 1950, when the Constitution had been introduced, to become India's sole national language.

The very first day of the Parliamentary Committee's meeting was so stormy that it seemed the Committee would break up sooner than later. Nearly all MPs from non-Hindi states wanted to reopen the Constitutional provision that Hindi would replace English. Hindi protagonists, with their name-plates in Hindi proudly placed next to their seats, said that the matter had been settled once and for all by the Constituent Assembly. This was true in a way. But the fact was that the Congress Parliamentary Party members in the assembly had voted at their own conclave in favour of Hindi by only one vote. Gyani Gurmukh Singh Musafir, a member from Punjab, had tilted the scales against English.

When I checked this with Pant, he said that the point of difference was whether numerals should be in Hindi or Roman. Musafir voted for Roman and hence the Constituent Assembly came to adopt that. I do not know if that is the full story. No book mentions it. The Congress has no record of the discussion which took place almost every evening among party members during the Constituent Assembly's sitting. Most decisions were taken at that meeting. The Constituent Assembly merely endorsed them.

The Home Ministry's note on the subject says: 'It would seem that general agreement had already been reached as regards the adoption of Hindi as the official language of the Union, and also on the other important provisions of the Constitution relating to language, before the discussion of the draft chapters relating to official language was taken up in the Constituent Assembly.' The main resolution was moved by the late Shri. N. Gopalaswami Ayyangar. In the discussion that followed, claims were advanced by different members in favour of Hindustani (it received only 16 votes); Bengali and Sanskrit being made the official language in place of Hindi, but the question of numerals – Devanagiri or international – occupied most of the time and attention of the members. Nehru was in favour of having Hindustani as India's language, a mixture of Hindi and Urdu, the language that Mahatma Gandhi spoke. But Sardar Patel, Nehru's number two, represented the crusty side of the party. His followers saw to it that Nehru's, or for that matter Gandhi's, wish was never fulfilled. Unlike Patel, Nehru did not want to rush things. This move fell through, because the Hindi supporters, in a hurry to switch over from English to Hindi, created a situation which almost endangered India's unity. Pant realized that, when the Parliamentary Committee finally met, the post-independence fervour to have one language as the focus of national unity, had ebbed. The criticism that Hindi had neither any cultural nor political preeminence over the other regional languages became louder. There was now a concerted effort to discuss the entire language question *de novo*.

Persons like C. Rajagopalachari who were once advocates of Hindi had been alienated by what they characterized as the 'vulgar haste' of Hindi supporters to 'impose' their language on others. He wanted English to continue; to maintain the status quo.

K.M. Munshi, one of the framers of the Constitution and a champion of Hindi, had warned the zealots that 'the pressure of propaganda as regards the time-limit should be relaxed in the interest of Hindi itself as well as the unity of India.' This had somewhat silenced them.

Yet, there was much resentment that the centre was bringing in Hindi 'through the backdoor'. The President's Order dated 27 May, 1952, authorizing the use of Hindi in addition to English for warrants of appointment of state governors and judges of the supreme and high courts had created only a minor flutter. But a greater stir followed an order issued on 3 December, 1965, allowing Hindi in correspondence with members of public and international organizations, in administrative reports, official journals and reports to parliament, government resolutions and legislative enactments, correspondence with state governments which had adopted Hindi as their official language, treaties and agreements, and government documents issued to diplomatic and consular officers and to Indian representations at international organizations. The non-Hindi-speaking people, who had regarded the switch-over as a far off possibility, genuinely feared that the centre was quickening the pace of its introduction. In a country where the government was the biggest provider of jobs, the fear and suspicion, however exaggerated, was not out of place.

The supporters of Hindi wanted to jettison English with immediate effect. They criticized the government for not doing enough for the proliferation and development of Hindi. And there were all kinds of pressures on the centre to introduce Hindi immediately in at least some spheres. The main argument for this was that some states were already imparting education in Hindi and it was unfair that students from these areas be asked to compete for government jobs in English, which they had not learnt or had learnt only cursorily.

Pant realized that the atmosphere was building up for two conflicting demands from the non-Hindi-speaking states for an indefinite postponement of the switch-over and from the Hindi-speaking states for a definite date for an early switch-over. Seven states had already adopted their regional language as the official language in place of English. It looked as though the remaining states would follow suit. The link between the different linguistic regions was already weakening.

English was still the only language stringing together north and south, east and west. But its standard was declining. The process of change-over to the Indian language media in education and in administration had accentuated the difficulty in finding recruits who could discharge their duties efficiently in English. A democratic government could not function indefinitely in a language which was understood by only a small fraction of the population. A common linguistic medium for communication among the different linguistic groups in India has to be from the soil; a country with its distinctive past and culture cannot continue to function indefinitely through a foreign medium. The protagonists of Hindi, who saw in the switch-over to the regional languages, indirect support for their cause, did not realize that this hurried change-over was really a threat to Hindi. The regional languages were taking the place which rightly belonged to Hindi. It was not realized that if and when Hindi came into its own as the only official language of the union it would not be able to push the regional languages out of the position; only a link language could do that.

Pant would often express such fears. But his main worry was how to end the fresh challenges to the settled issue of Hindi as the official language of the union. He could see that by not insisting on a definite date for the change-over and not restricting the use of English, he could head off the demand for new thinking on the language question. He realized that the switch-over to Hindi would be postponed indefinitely. He adopted the course of not pushing Hindi, even at the expense of annoying the supporters of Hindi. In all the sittings of the Parliamentary Committee spread over sixteen months, he leaned heavily towards the non-Hindi-speaking members. Never did he go against their wishes, especially their spokesman, Mosur Kandasami Mudaliar. The result was that Pant was able to get the Committee to endorse the Constitutional obligation of having Hindi as the official language of the India union.

~

Home Minister Gobind Ballabh Pant was unhappy that the proceedings of the Parliamentary Language Committee were appearing in print. He feared that if this were to continue, the controversial language debate would become a national issue, endlessly engaging the attention of the entire country and provoking a similar discussion to be mirrored in the media. This would revive the language issue and open the way to renewed questioning of the status of Hindi. The status of Hindi might come to be questioned all over again, he feared.

The Constituent Assembly had agreed much earlier that Hindi would be India's official language. All that remained to be settled, was whether it would be formally introduced on 26 January 1965, or on some later date, to enable non-Hindi-speaking people time to learn it.

Pant made personal requests to the Committee members not to brief the press. A few refused. Prominent among them was Frank Anthony, an Anglo-Indian member of parliament. His contention was that the matter was too serious to be kept from the public. Pant was distraught and helpless. I, the information officer, was asked to tell newspapers not to report what members said about the Committee's proceedings. I conveyed Pant's request to Delhi editors and senior correspondents, asking them not to publish what the Committee members said at their meeting. The press refused to provide the assurance requested. Then I had a brainwave. I warned the pressmen that the proceedings of the Committee were privileged. This was not true. Only a Standing Committee enjoyed such a privilege, not a Committee constituted by the House. I told the press that reporting the Committee's proceedings would amount to a breach of privilege.

The trick worked. No pressmen checked with the parliament secretariat whether my contention was correct. Later, some Committee members complained to Pant telling him about how I had misled the press; he kept quiet. Nothing appeared in the press on the Committee's deliberations till the end, although the meetings spread over a span of one and a half years.

After the report was released, I offered my apologies to the pressmen and told them that the Committee's proceedings had no status of privilege. They were furious and, literally, abused me. What hurt them most was that they had been hoodwinked. They took up the matter with Pant who said that he would check with me. Instead, he thanked me. Whether what I did was ethically correct, I would leave to the judgement of the pressmen concerned. For my part, I was convinced that the day-to-day reporting on the Committee's deliberations would reopen the question of whether Hindi was suitable to become the Indian union's language.

In fact, the Committee members were so divided on this issue that it was a tribute to Pant's patience and tact that he was able to get a unanimous report: it was decided that Hindi would be the principal language and English the subsidiary one, with no target date set for the switch-over.

Pant took one more precaution to stop any further discussion on the status of Hindi being India's language: he stopped the appointment of subsequent commissions. The Constitution had laid down that after every ten years a commission would be appointed to find out how far Hindi had spread, so that a complete switch over from English could take place. Following his experience of the Committee's deliberations, he realized that the very basis of Hindi as the union's language would come to be questioned if there were to be another commission.

On the insistence of Pant, both the Home and Law Ministries 'studied' the Constitutional position and came to the conclusion that the word 'shall' could be interpreted as 'may'. Therefore, the president was not bound to appoint a commission every ten years. The government acted accordingly. Another commission, which was due in 1960, was never constituted – indeed none has been since then.

However, the interpretation of the word 'shall' as 'may' gave C.N. Annadurai, of the Dravida Munnetra Kazhagam

(DMK) an opportunity to plead with Nehru for the retention of English. His plea was that 'may' could be substituted with 'shall' to permit the use of English in addition to Hindi beyond 1965. In his reply, Nehru said that he was prepared to retain English as an associate language or an alternative language until otherwise decided by non-Hindi-speaking people. But he saw no way how he could make this provision in the statute.

Subsequently, when the pro-English sentiment became stronger in the south, a change of phraseology was demanded. The pertinent Clause 3 of the Language Act said: 'Notwithstanding the expiration of the period of fifteen years from the commencement of the Constitution, the English language may, as from the appointed day, continue to be used, in addition to Hindi – (a) for all the official purposes of the union for which it was being used immediately before that day; and (b) for the transaction of business in parliament.'

By the time the Language Bill was passed, some states which had adopted Hindi as their regional language were anxious to introduce it for high court judgements. The bill authorized the governor, after consulting the president, to allow the use of Hindi or the official language of the states, in addition to English, 'for any judgement, decree or order passed or made by the high court of that state'.

To satisfy the Hindi-speaking population, the Bill laid down that the president 'may appoint a committee' to review the progress made in the use of Hindi. But there was no mention of reconstitution of the commission lest the entire matter be reopened. When the bill was discussed, MPs from non-Hindi-speaking areas reminded Nehru of his undertaking that he would leave it to them to decide when to switch over to Hindi. They wanted to amend the Constitution accordingly.

The government promised to implement Nehru's assurance, but did not say when or how. There was, however, an influential section in the government which was not serious about it. But there were some who sincerely believed that such assurances were difficult to legislate. The passage of time was thought to be the best solution; no action was taken. Consequently, some doubt about the real intentions of the centre continued to exist in the mind of the non-Hindi-speaking population.

An overzealous home minister, Gulzarilal Nanda, under Prime Minister Lal Bahadur Shastri, gave a fresh lease of life to the language controversy. He issued a circular that Hindi would become the principal language of the Indian union on 26 January, 1965 and that English would be an additional language, to be used for all purposes.

In another circular, the Home Ministry said a beginning should be made by giving Hindi names to central government offices, organizations and institutions in addition to their English ones. To start with, central government offices constituted in Hindi-speaking states were to be given Hindi names. Thereafter, the process of the change-over to Indian names would be carried on steadily. The Home Ministry also asked all the ministries to transcribe all government forms, rules and manuals into Hindi.

Madras state was perturbed by the circular. After all, language touched the livelihood of the people, and they feared that their chances of employment in government jobs would be adversely affected once Hindi became the major language. State-wide agitation started building up in January – February 1965. Nanda's assurance that the introduction of Hindi would be so regulated as not to cause any hardship to the non-Hindi-speaking people did not stop the agitation from spreading and becoming violent. One after another, five people set their clothes on fire and immolated themselves in Madras.

First, the government blamed the DMK for 'exploiting the people's ignorance about the exact position on the official language'. Later, the existence of the circular itself was denied. Utimately, the Home Ministry asked ministers not to issue any circular but to wait for 'comprehensive instructions on the subject'. That was never done; eventually, the Home Ministry had burnt its fingers so badly that it did not do anything with regard to Hindi any more.

The riots came to an end, but the confidence of the non-Hindi-speaking people was shattered beyond redemption. The Congress leaders from the south took upon themselves the task of voicing the fears of these groups. The trio – K. Kamaraj, Neelam Sanjeeva Reddy and S. Nijalingappa (with Atulya Ghosh) approached Lal Bahadur Shastri to devise ways of allaying their fear. C.N. Annadurai wanted an amendment to the Constitution to keep the use of Hindi in abeyance indefinitely. C. Rajagopalachari wanted English to be 'imposed' on the country for all time. This was not the position of Kamaraj and others. They were against 'hurry,' not against Hindi which, Kamaraj said in a public statement had been chosen to be 'a common language to maintain the unity of the country politically and administratively'. Shastri readily issued a statement saying that the switch-over to Hindi would be further slowed down, but he kept quiet about implementing Nehru's assurances. Shastri was under great pressure from the Hindi lobby in parliament not to agree to bilingualism for an indefinite period. Personally he favoured an early introduction of Hindi because, unlike Nehru, he felt more at home with Hindi. But sensing the mood of the south, he favoured an all-party consensus on the switch-over date.

When no specific move to give legal shape to the assurances of Nehru was made, the south started an agitation. Students in Madras began to protest against the imposition of Hindi. By that time, the schools and colleges in the state had reopened. The situation was building up to a climax.

The Madras agitation took a violent turn: in one day, on 10 February 1965, 19 people were killed by police bullets and two sub-inspectors were burnt to death. Troops moved to trouble spots. Shastri realized that his prevarication had caused harm. He broadcast an announcement to non-Hindi-speaking people. A cabinet meeting was convened on 11 February to finalize the statement, which said that Nehru's assurances 'will be honoured in letter and in spirit without any qualification or reservation'. The nation was saved from a conflagration.

7

After Nehru: The Fight for Succession

JAWAHARLAL NEHRU FELL IN THE BATHROOM AND DIED A FEW hours later in his bed. When his personal physician, K.L.Wig, was summoned in the early hours on 27 May, 1964, he expressed his dismay about the fact that Nehru had been allowed to walk without any person supporting him, despite his strict orders to that effect. Mrs Indira Gandhi and the night nurse had dozed off.

By Nehru's bedside were the Gita and the Upanishads. In fact, he always carried the Gita in his briefcase along with an abridged version of the UN Charter. According to his cabinet minister, Tiruvallur Thattai Krishnamachari, popularly known as TTK, Nehru had 'become religious' in his last days – this was the same person who had refused in 1954 to go into a south Indian temple when asked to take his shirt off. For a person who had said that he had no faith in rites and rituals, his funeral was a high-caste Hindu ceremony; for a person who had consecrated secularism in the Indian Constitution, it was a sectarian cremation; for a person who was an agnostic, it was a religious farewell.

K. Kamaraj was the Congress president when Nehru died. It was he who had to find a successor. All eyes were on him.

Lal Bahadur Shastri and Morarji Desai were the two obvious choices. TTK thought that his proximity to Nehru would make him the successor, at least for an 'interim period' till the obvious choice emerged, but he was never in the reckoning. Gulzarilal Nanda, officiating as prime minister till the party decided on the successor, had no chance either; Kamaraj did not take him seriously.

Shastri's plus point was that he was considered Nehru's protégé. He had been inducted as minister without portfolio after Nehru suffered a stroke in Bhubaneswar in January 1964. Both TTK and Nanda had opposed the inclusion of Shastri. TTK told me that Nehru had once described Shastri 'as a small and cunning man who would stab you in the back'. But none – and I talked to many – believed that Pandjitji, as Nehru was affectionately called, could have used such words for anybody, much less for Shastri whom he liked. However, former foreign minister, Dinesh Singh, who was then close to the Nehru household, recalled during a talk with me on 5 April, 1973: 'Pandjitji was capable of saying harsh things. For example, when Indiraji insisted on bringing back Durga Prasad Mishra as Madhya Pradesh chief minister, Panditji said, "*Woh admi achha nahin hai*" (that man is not good). Panditji was fond of intelligent men. It is quite possible that he might have used the words TTK repeated.'

But there is no doubt that Kamaraj preferred Shastri. He considered him above the influence of 'big money', something he could not vouch for, for Morarji Desai. Kamaraj had another obligation to fulfil. A few weeks earlier he had met some provincial party leaders, including S. Nijalingappa from Karnataka, Atulya Ghosh from West Bengal and Neelam Sanjeeva Reddy from Andhra Pradesh, in the temple town of Tirupati. They had all agreed on Shastri as the successor to Nehru – who by then had had a stroke in Bhubaneshwar.

Even before Kamaraj started the process of finding India's next prime minister from within the Congress party, Morarji alleged that Kamaraj was not an honest broker and that he had already made up his mind to nominate Shastri. To Kamaraj's surprise, he found most leftists within the Congress on Morarji's side. For example, two former central ministers with leftist leanings supported Morarji. One, Krishna Menon, later told me that he did not support Morarji at any time and that he had wanted Gulzarilal Nanda to be prime minister 'as an interim arrangement'. And the other, Keshav Dev Malaviya, said in an interview that 'we would have voted for Shastri, not Morarji, if it ever came to a contest'. Their attitude, as well as that of the Communist Party of India, spread the impression that the USSR preferred Morarji to Shastri. Moscow meant a lot in those days because the Socialist pattern was the ideology India followed.

Indira Gandhi was not in the picture. However, Shastri said that he favoured a consensus candidate and mentioned her name, along with that of Jayaprakash Narayan's. He did not want the election but if there were to be one, he was clear, he could defeat Morarji, not Indira Gandhi.

A few months before Nehru's death I had relinquished my post as information officer to Shastri, to head the United News of India (UNI). In fact, the election of Nehru's successor was my first major political story after quitting the Press Information Bureau (PIB) of the central government.

After Nehru, who? Any journalist would have followed the same lead. To find the answer, I went first to Shastri's house. It was his routine to pace up and down in his lawn, meeting visitors one by one and talking and walking at the same time. He saw me and indicated with a wave of his hand that I should come back later. I learned that he was going to Nehru's cremation site to see what to do because Nehru's body had not burnt fully – for a thin man he had large bones.

The contest for prime ministership appeared inevitable. Congressmen did not want it because they feared that the division would split the party. They had enjoyed a togetherness in the security of Nehru's leadership and wished the same unity to prevail. Kamaraj was conscious of this. He tried to bring Morarji around, so that he would not force an election for the leader, but he was determined to do so. From Shastri's place I drove straight to Morarji's residence. This was the first time I met his son, Kanti Desai. He was standing with the then deputy finance minister, Tarakeswari Sinha, brandishing a list which I soon discovered was that of Congress MPs. Both knew that I had worked with Shastri, but both also knew that I had left him to join the UNI. Still they called me Shastri's man to my face. 'Shastri's man,' Tarakeswari Sinha said, 'you better tell Shastri to withdraw from the field because the majority of MPs are supporting us.'

I had met Tarakeswari Sinha earlier through our common friend, the late railway minister Lalit Nayaran Mishra. I conveyed to Kanti Desai Shastri's wish to avoid the contest and have a consensus candidate, and that he would agree to the name of either Jayaprakash Narayan or Indira Gandhi. (When Morarji heard about this, subsequently, he did not say anything about JP but dismissed Indira Gandhi as 'that chit of a girl'). Kanti Desai made it clear that if there had to be a consensus candidate, it would be none other than his father. He showed me the list on which he had ticked off the names of MPs who had 'promised' to vote for Morarji. On paper, they had a majority.

When I found Kanti Desai going on record to say that his father would fight for the leadership if he was not nominated, I thought I had the making of a story. I went back to Shastri. He reiterated that he was opposed to any election and still favoured a consensus. There were two stances: Morarji's categorical; Shastri's equivocal.

I wrote the story thus:

Mr Morarji Desai, former finance minister, is the first one to throw his hat into the ring. He is believed to have told his associates that he is a candidate. Mr Desai is understood to have said that there must be an election to find out who has the majority. He said he would not withdraw from the field in any case ... Circles close to Shastri said that he would like to avoid a contest as far as possible and would be ready to step down in favour of a candidate who would have the unanimous support of the party...

Having earned a masters degree in journalism from the US, I had picked up some American clichés. The phrase, 'to throw the hat into the ring' was not generally used by the Indian press. But I used it to convey that Morarji was the first one to announce his candidature. Shastri came out well in the story because he was willing to accept a consensus candidate.

Fresh from the government information department, I had never imagined the impact of the printed word. I experienced it when I went to the Central Hall of Parliament. As I was going up the stairs of Parliament House, Kamaraj was coming down. He embraced me and whispered, 'Thank you'. Before I could say anything, he had disappeared into his car. I was baffled.

In Central Hall, several MPs told me that my story had cost Morarji at least 100 votes. Morarji's haste to enforce an election had evoked widespread criticism. There was also some revulsion that Morarji had declared himself as a candidate even before 'the ashes of Nehru had got cold'. Morarji came across as ambitious and selfish in comparison to the self-effacing, withdrawn Shastri. When I returned to my office, I found Shastri's house had called me many a time and had left messages to meet him immediately. I rushed to his house. He saw me from afar and left his other visitors to grab my hand to say: 'No more stories. It is all done.' I was taken aback by the remark. Had I helped Shastri unwittingly? This thought nagged me then and it still does. It seemed to me that my story had hurt Morarji and benefitted Shastri's image.

In the meanwhile, the Congress high command found a way to avoid the election. Kamaraj was entrusted with the task of finding out each Congress member's view and preference. The Rajya Sabha MPs were included. Support for Shastri was overwhelming. He was elected to lead the party.

Morarji never accepted Kamaraj's decision. Nor did he believe that the story I did was not designed to help Shastri. Although I met him to apologize for having hurt him, albeit unwittingly, his reply was that Shastri had 'a way of getting things done'. He never forgave me. He remembered the story even after he became prime minister in 1977, nearly thirteen years after the story had appeared.

But now I realize that I had helped Shastri unwittingly. I got evidence of this fact within a few days of Shastri's becoming the prime minister. He asked me to rejoin him as his press attaché. I said I would like to take up the position provided he made me his press secretary, the status which Jim Haggerty enjoyed during US president Truman's presidential term.

Shastri said: 'If I were to do so, Morarji would say that I have repaid your debt!'

Shastri's
Prime Ministership

8

The First Stirrings of War

'YOU WERE FOOLED BY OUR MESSAGES, BELIEVING THAT WE HAD moved the artillery to the Sialkot sector,' General Tikka Khan, former commander-in-chief of Pakistan, told me when I met him several years after the 1965 war between India and Pakistan. 'We had no artillery to move because we had stationed it elsewhere. You could have walked into Sialkot without any resistance.'

This was correct. However, General J.N. Chaudhari, who was the Indian chief of army staff at that time, had a different story to tell. He said that during the last World War he had seen how a large Russian army had been pinned down by Berlin for fourteen days in a bid to occupy the capital of Nazi Germany. 'I did not want that to happen,' he told me.

This, indeed, might have been the case. Still, the occupation of Sialkot would have given a message to the world that India had proved its prowess by winning the war. With neither Sialkot nor Lahore under India's control, the 1965 war was, at best, a 60 per cent victory for New Delhi if not a draw. It was primarily a war of attrition – with New Delhi destroying a large number of Islamabad's weapons, particularly the Patton tanks which America had given it for being a member of the CENTO (Central Treaty Organization) and the SEATO (South East Asia Treaty Organization) – the two military arrangements against the Soviet Bloc during the Cold War.

I visited the Sialkot sector after the ceasefire. Seeing the spire of the city's church I remembered how I had passed by it last when I had left Sialkot, my hometown, as a refugee, on 13 September, 1947. I was then twenty years old. I had not realized when I had left it that time that there would be no coming back. This realization dawned only when I hit the Grand Trunk road and joined the sea of humanity, largely moving towards India, with people hugging their few belongings and their memories.

Partition took a terrible toll. One million people lost their lives and another twenty million were rendered homeless.

One picture from that time is etched vividly in my mind: I was nearing Lahore. It was still daylight. I saw people huddled into trucks and on foot passing me in the opposite direction. They were Muslims with the same pain-etched faces as us — men and women with their luggage bundled on their heads and their fear-stricken children trailing behind. They, too, had left behind their hearths and homes, friends and hopes. I stood in silence watching them; only watching them. I did not speak nor did they. But we understood each other; it was a spontaneous kinship. Both had seen murder and worse; both had been broken on the rack of history; both were refugees.

The 1965 war, which broke out in September, was really a sequel to the hostilities in the Rann of Kutch a few months earlier, in April. This was over a territory, 3500 square miles, in western Gujarat. It had remained undemarcated. Even the Radcliffe Award was silent on it. The Indian mission in Pakistan had warned New Delhi that the Rann of Kutch operation was just a rehearsal and that a bigger attack was possible elsewhere. Documents captured in August 1965 from the two Pakistani army captains, Ghulam Hussain and Mohammed Sajjad, clearly indicated Rawalpindi's plan: the Rann of Kutch operation on the one hand and the starting of the recruitment of infiltrators to fight in Kashmir, on the other.

Harold Wilson, then British prime minister, intervened to stop hostilities by talking to both Prime Minister Lal Bahadur Shastri and President Ayub Khan, both of whom were in London to attend the Commonwealth Prime Ministers' Conference. There was an immediate ceasefire with a provision for ministerial-level talks. It was agreed that if the talks did not bring about a compromise, a tribunal would demarcate the boundary. The ministerial meeting never took place; Pakistan did not reply to India's communication or to subsequent reminders. Consequently, a tribunal was appointed and it awarded the territory to Pakistan.

At the height of the Rann of Kutch dispute, New Delhi noticed that Moscow tended to take a neutral position. The Soviet Union expressed the hope that India and Pakistan would both display restraint and settle their disputes between themselves, taking into consideration each other's natural interests. In fact, New Delhi's feeling was that after Nehru's death (May, 1964) and more so after Nikita Khrushchev's exit (October, 1964), the Soviet Union was inclined to sit on the fence.

Shastri did approach Moscow for support on the Rann of Kutch but it was reluctant to say anything in public. However, the Russian leaders reiterated their full support on Kashmir, offered more military equipment and promised to double trade, which in 1964 totalled $253.7 million both ways. I remember Alexei Kosygin telling us – the six journalists covering Shastri's Soviet visit – that India and Pakistan should not allow 'imperialists' to drive a wedge between them.

As Pakistan had planned, it sent infiltrators into Kashmir once the Rann of Kutch operation was over. The Rawalpindi calculation was that there would be uprisings in the Kashmir valley. They were wrong. In fact, two Kashmiri shepherds – Mohammed Din and Wazir Mohammed – were the first to inform the Kashmir police about the infiltration. Pakistan's plans to distribute arms and ammunition to the local population and to organize a revolt remained on paper. On 1 September,1965 General Ayub Khan, in a radio broadcast, said that by supporting the people of Kashmir to exercise their right of self-determination, Pakistan was doing no more than what it had always pledged. He asked the Kashmiris to rise as one man. When Ayub heard that there was no response to his call, his contemptuous comment was that he knew all about the 'mentality' of Kashmiris. It was Zulfikar Ali Bhutto, then foreign minister, who had misinformed him.

When I met Ayub at his residence in Islamabad early in 1972 after the Bangladesh War he told me that the 1965 war was Bhutto's war and I should ask him about it. Bhutto told me that he had no regrets about having persuaded Ayub to send in the infiltrators. 'If I know anything about the Kashmiris, they will never raise the gun,' Ayub told me. He did not live to see the day when the uprising in Kashmir did take place, beginning in 1988.

Pakistan followed the infiltration with a massive attack on 1 September 1965 in the Chhamb sector of Jammu. Now Shastri had no choice. He had to attack Pakistan to relieve pressure in the area. Had he not done so, Kashmir would have been cut off from India. He told his military commanders that Indian forces should be in Lahore before the fall of Chhamb.

That very day Shastri allowed the execution of Operation Riddle. Four days later, Indian forces began a three-pronged advance into Pakistan. Ayub reportedly said subsequently that if he had known that the Chhamb action meant war, he would never have allowed it. Probably, he thought that India would never cross the recognized international border. But he was wrong in his calculations because, since Nehru's days, New Delhi had made it clear that an attack on Kashmir would mean an attack on India.

'Who ordered the forces to march towards Pakistan?' I once asked Shastri.

'I', he replied.

'What would Panditji, your father, have done in these circumstances?' I once asked Indira Gandhi.

'He would have done the same as Shastriji did. It was the decision of the military commanders which Shastri endorsed.' (Y.B. Chavan, then defence minister, tended to agree with what Mrs Gandhi said.)

When I posed to Pakistan's authorities the question as to whether Nehru would have allowed Indian forces to cross the international border, the reply was in the negative; Bhutto agreed with the assessment. Krishna Menon told me that Nehru would not have gone to war. Menon quoted Nehru as saying that he had too many problems and that he would not like to take on Pakistan. Also, Menon said, Nehru was against Hindu communalism. 'War with Pakistan would have created problems internally on the Hindu–Muslim front.'

What Nehru would have done if he had been alive in 1965 is difficult to say. But there is no doubt that his thinking was different and he was fully convinced that a war between India and Pakistan would spell ruin for the subcontinent. He always talked of 'the folly of war' between the two countries if it ever took place.

9

Dealing with the Infiltrators

ZULFIKAR ALI BHUTTO DID NOT DENY THE INFILTRATION. HE was not even apologetic about the 1965 war. He defended himself by arguing that he started the war because of the manner in which India's war machine had been gearing up. He said he thought that if Pakistan ever had a chance, it was in 1965.

The infiltration was an interesting story to pursue. It must have required large-scale planning as is clear from Pakistan's action in Kargil. Browsing through Pakistani newspapers of that time, I stumbled upon a presidential ordinance which Islamabad had promulgated on the Mujahid – volunteers for holy war.

This authorized the government to formally constitute a force of jehadis and train it. This was the beginning of the training of militants. Major General Akhtar Malik was given free charge of this operation in May, 1965.

The Pakistan plan was to arrange for the infiltration of these terrorists into Kashmir in small groups and for them to converge into the valley from various directions between the first and the fifth of August. The militants were expected to mingle unnoticed with the thousands of people congregating on 8 August for celebrating the festival of Dastagir Sahib, a local sufi.

The militants were to join the demonstration in Srinagar on the first anniversary of Sheikh Abdullah's detention, stage an armed revolt and capture in the process the radio station, the airfield and other vital centres. A few other columns of infiltrators were to block the roads connecting Srinagar with other parts of the state so as to isolate the capital.

Subsequently, the raiders were to form a 'revolutionary council', proclaim themselves a lawful government and broadcast an appeal for recognition and assistance from all countries, especially Pakistan. (A copy of the proclamation of the war of liberation was to be broadcast by Radio Kashmir on 9 August). The 'broadcast' was to be the signal for Pakistan to move in for the kill.

The early detection of the infiltrators only accentuated the pace of events. There was a spate of serious incursions throughout Jammu and Kashmir, all aimed at capturing the valley. It appeared as if the militants had been assigned special jobs like the destruction of bridges, the disruption of lines of communication, attacks on military formations and the distribution of arms and ammunition to local civilian sympathizers.

The invaders set about their task with missionary zeal and were confident of a spontaneous response from the masses whom they had come to 'liberate'. But the local population kept itself aloof. On 8 August the infiltrators managed to enter one of the suburbs of Srinagar. The state government became so panicky that it asked Delhi to impose martial law in the state. Accordingly, the central government asked the army to take control of the entire state. The army commanders, however, dissuaded the government from doing so and assured them that the situation was not as bad as was depicted by the state government.

On the night of 8 August, for the first time, the whole of the ceasefire line burst into flame with intensive and continuous fire across the border. In the Poonch area Pakistan shelled selected targets with 25-pounder guns. The infiltrators – roughly 3000 in the state – made a daring raid on Brigade Headquarters but there were no casualties.

At the same time, Pakistan was at great pains to explain through the press and radio, that the happenings in Jammu and Kashmir were 'a spontaneous local insurrection' in which it had no hand.

During the night of 9 August there was a comparative lull in the valley. That very night some infiltrators were fired upon as they tried to slip back into Pakistan. This was the first indication of infiltrator traffic in the reverse direction.

Lieutenant General Harbaksh Singh, chief of Western Command, described the scene at Srinagar to me thus:

> The streets were deserted and there were visible signs of anxiety and tension on the faces of the residents gaping through the windows! On the night of the twelfth, Srinagar was still ringing with intermittent fire throughout the city. The ceasefire line was also kept ablaze by Pakistan and in the Poonch sector an ammunition dump was almost on the point of falling into the infiltrators' hands when Indian troops with artillery support stepped into the breach and drove them away.

Once the infiltrators met with resistance, they withdrew. The operation failed. In his report to New Delhi, Harbaksh Singh said:

> The Pakistanis borrowed a leaf from the teachings of Mao Tse-tung in their plan for instigating an insurrection in J&K under the guise of a spontaneous 'Liberation Movement'. But it was in the implementation of the Chinese doctrine on the subject

that Pakistani leadership faulted and fell. To succeed in this form of subversive warfare, it requires meticulous organization, detailed planning, a high standard of training, aggressive leadership and complete local support. Without these basic essentials a liberation movement is bound to fizzle out – as it did in J&K.

On 14 -15 August, Harbaksh Singh, after getting New Delhi's permission through a hurried telephone call, captured two Pakistani posts – Point 13620 and Saddle – overlooking mountainous Kargil. The posts posed a threat to the line of communication in that sector.

The occupation of the two posts did not satisfy Indian parliament members; they wanted the government to chase the infiltrators across the ceasefire line. Y.B. Chavan promised (23 August) to the Lok Sabha that they would do so 'if necessary'.

In fact, that necessity arose a few days later. On 25 August, Indian forces crossed the ceasefire line in the Uri sector to prevent concentration of infiltrators in that area. The Pakistani forces, which had been making inroads into the Chhamb sector in Jammu since 5 August now attacked from the Gilgit side. The attack made on 28 August was near Gurez, one of the gateways from the north to the Kashmir valley. The Pakistani forces were repulsed.

Islamabad tried more or less the same thing subsequently, through infiltrators in July, 2005. In the Uri sector, Indian forces continued their advance and penetrated up to Haji Pir, a strategic mountain pass at a height of 8,600 feet which the infiltrators used as one of the main points of ingress. (Haji Pir is the nerve centre of Pakistan's road communication for the entire area.) Earlier, Indian forces had occupied the heights overlooking Tithwal, another dominant feature.

With the capture of Haji Pir, the routes taken by the infiltrators and the Pakistan Army were plugged. However,

Rawalpindi described India's gain as an attempt to 'rehabilitate their sagging morale because the world knows about their debacle in Kutch'.

Meanwhile, New Delhi increased its diplomatic activity to whip up world opinion against infiltration from Pakistan. B.K. Nehru, then India's envoy in Washington, met Dean Rusk, then US secretary of state, and explained – as other Indian envoys did to leaders of the countries to which they were accredited – that Pakistani Army officers were leading 'massive infiltration' and causing violations of the ceasefire line. Rawalpindi explained that no Pakistani soldier was involved. Kewal Singh, then Indian high commissioner to Pakistan, met Bhutto who said it was only an 'uprising' in Jammu and Kashmir.

The UN secretary general, to whom India complained, described the situation as 'a dangerous threat to peace' but did nothing beyond summoning for consultations, Lieutenant General R.H. Nimmo, head of the United Nations Military Observer Group in Kashmir. His interpretation was that the ceasefire agreement applied only to armed forces on either side and not to civilians, armed or unarmed. However, in his report on 5 August, he confirmed the crossing of the ceasefire line by Pakistani armed infiltrators in an attempt to destroy strategic points of communication. *Pravda* said on 24 August, in an editorial that Kashmir was 'an integral part of India' and hoped that a settlement of the present situation in Kashmir would be brought about peacefully between India and Pakistan.

Kosygin wrote to Shastri that 'the rights and wrongs of the present situation were hardly of any importance at the moment... The main efforts should be concentrated on the immediate termination of military operations and to stop tanks and silence the guns'. His letter was not at all pro-India and it equated New Delhi with Rawalpindi for playing into the hands of 'American imperialism'.

Pakistan's action, after the intrusion in the Rann of Kutch, had driven India towards hawks who said that Pakistan must be taught a lesson. Rawalpindi launched a heavy attack on 1 September in the Akhnur-Jammu sector by crossing the ceasefire line and a small portion of the international border. This made up Shastri's mind.

Two days later – 3 September – Shastri ordered the Indian Army to march into Pakistan. The actual attack came on 6 September. It would have come a day earlier but the Indian Air Force wanted to pound the 'enemy' bases first; it hardly did so. In fact, the Pakistan Air Force attacked Pathankot airport on the 6th afternoon and destroyed thirteen Indian planes.

After the war, Shastri told me, 'Chaudhuri (the chief of the army staff) and the others were taken aback when I asked them to march into Pakistan.'

Harbaksh Singh told me that the army could never forget 'this tallest decision by the shortest man'.

(Shastri was about five feet tall!)

10

The Counter-attack

PRIME MINISTER LAL BAHADUR SHASTRI HAD VERY LITTLE choice. The Indian troops were greatly outnumbered and out-positioned in the Chhamb sector and on the Poonch –Rajouri and the Jammu – Srinagar road. This was the only link with the valley and it was threatened.

If the road were to be cut off, all Indian forces in Jammu and Kashmir would be isolated. Indian units were operating in difficult terrain in that area and could only use light tanks while Pakistan was able to move in the heaviest tanks.

'I want to reach Lahore before they take Srinagar,' Shastri told our chief of army staff, General J.N. Chaudhuri.

The army headquarters actually prepared a plan to attack Pakistan at the time of the Kutch confrontation, when the two countries had almost reached the point of war. In fact, a few days earlier, General Chaudhuri had told Lieutenant General Harbaksh Singh, who was heading the Northern Command, that India, should be ready to attack Pakistan across the international border within 48 hours when there was a new challenge.

This was what happened –

Harbaksh Singh told General Chaudhuri that India must move towards Pakistan if it ever 'marched' on Kashmir.

Therefore, when Chhamb was attacked – and Pakistan crossed nearly a quarter of a mile of the international border in the process – he repeated Jawaharlal Nehru's warning that any attack on Kashmir was an attack on India. Harbaksh Singh's argument for marching into Pakistan made sense militarily as it served to relieve pressure. It looked difficult to hold Kashmir the way Pakistani forces were advancing in the Chhamb sector.

'Operation Riddle' was the codeword for the attack fixed for 4 a.m. on 6 September 1965. A three-pronged thrust was mounted from Amritsar, Ferozepur and Gurdaspur, and two days later on 8 September, the Sialkot front was opened. (Sialkot was the base from where Pakistan had planned an attack on the Chhamb sector.)

It was not that Pakistan had ruled out an Indian offensive across the international border. Reliable reports reaching New Delhi indicated that Rawalpindi had moved the major elements of its Armoured Division (approximately two Patton regiments) into the Lahore area. In addition, most of 8 Infantry Division from Peshawar had been moved to the Lyallpur–Sheikhupura area, with one of its brigades at Marala Headworks, about 25 miles from Sialkot. Harbaksh Singh's own expectation was that Pakistan would adopt an aggressive defensive posture in the Punjab and Rajasthan sectors.

Still, there was an element of surprise for Pakistan in the timing of the attack; Indian forces advanced in all sectors without much resistance. By 9 a.m. India had occupied Pakistan's defence positions in the Ichhogil canal, five miles from the border in the Ferozepur sector, the Dera Baba Nanak bridge in the Gurdaspur sector, and the same Ichhogil canal which was ten miles from the Amritsar–Wagah border in the Lahore sector.

By 10.30 a.m. one column in the Lahore sector had crossed the Ichhogil canal and reached a little beyond the Bata shoe factory on the outskirts of Lahore city.

The Pakistan Air Force attacked this column many a time and destroyed 100 vehicles in a couple of hours.

Major General Niranjan Prasad, commanding the sector, sent an SOS informing his Corps headquarters that he had given orders to his men to withdraw by seven miles. The reason he gave was that half of the vehicles of his division (nearly 20,000 vehicles) had been destroyed. He also mentioned the attack by the Pakistan armour on the flanks.

Harbaksh Singh, who happened to be at Corps headquarters, munching a sandwich and feeling on top of the world at the time because everything was going according to plan, said later that he got very angry when he heard this. He ordered Prasad not to withdraw the men. But by then the worst had happened. The advance column retreated in confusion with much loss to life and equipment. Prasad was removed. His withdrawal cost India heavily. It took our forces more than a fortnight to reach even the Ichhogil canal and that too after a heavy loss of men and material.

By the night of 10 September, Indian forces in the Ferozepore sector reached Burki but had to cool their heels because their advance was linked with the progress in the Sialkot sector where the stalemate continued till the ceasefire was ordered at 3.30 a.m. on 23 September.

The real fighting took place in the Khem Karan sector where Pakistan troops planned to cut off the Grand Trunk road at Jandial Guru near Amritsar and capture the vital bridges at Beas and Harika. The area had been obviously chosen with care because it was just plain countryside without many canals and waterways.

For two days the battle was grim. On 10 September, Chaudhuri called Harbaksh Singh to Ambala and suggested the withdrawal of forces to the banks of the Beas – 60 miles inside Indian territory – so as to have a natural barrier to stop Pakistan's forces.

Harbaksh Singh, or more so his corps commander, Dhillon, refused to carry out the plan. In truth, it was never executed. (Chaudhuri denied this during his talk with me. He said: 'Those who know me also know that I don't tolerate any nonsense or disobedience from my army commanders.')

However, that was the last encounter between the two generals. Chaudhuri, an armoured hand, told Harbaksh Singh, an infantry man, that he did not understand armour; Harbaksh Singh said it was courage that mattered, not technical knowledge. After this meeting their relationship was only cursory.

By the time Harbaksh Singh returned from Ambala, the Indian forces had foiled Pakistan's thrust into the Khem Karan sector. But they did little to consolidate their gains. Pakistan got the time it needed to revise its strategy accordingly.

In his assessment to the government, Harbaksh Singh later said:

It was fortunate too that Pakistan failed in her grand design in the Khem Karan sector. A blitzkrieg deep into our territory towards the G.T. road or the Beas bridge would have left us in the helpless position of a commander paralysed into inaction for want of readily available reserves while the enemy was inexorably pushing deep into his vitals. It is a nightmarish feeling even when considered in retrospect at this stage.

The terrain in the Khem Karan sector helped India. Pakistan's tanks had to line up to meet Indian forces which were secure on three sides: the river on one side, the canal on the second and a railway track on the third. And then the US-supplied Patton tanks were too sophisticated for the average Pakistani soldier to handle. Computers often went wrong; the tank crews fed incorrect information into the electronic brain and the gunner usually got so involved that he rarely had the chance to fire before the rough and ready gunnery of India's older, simpler and less complicated armour would knock his tank off. This might sound like a paradox but the sheer modernity of the Patton was its undoing.

Brigadier Theograj, who commanded armour at Phillaur (the Khem Karan sector), later said that he never thought that he was fighting against an entire armoured division; he believed the first Pattons he encountered were stray ones. 'Had I known that it was an armoured division, I might have retreated,' he said. However, the fact remained that he knocked off more than 100 Pattons. The canal, breached by India, provided the slush in which most of the tanks got stuck.

After repulsing Pakistan's armour in the Khem Karan sector, Harbaksh Singh tried to bolster Indian armour in the Sialkot sector. The plan was to surround Sialkot and declare it an open city. But India had lost the initiative on this front. After covering a distance of five to seven miles, Indian forces could not go further because of Pakistan's continuous shelling, and what Harbaksh Singh characterized as, 'the lack of drive on the part of Indian commanders'.

Rawalpindi diverted part of the armoured division from the Khem Karan sector to Sialkot. Or so it was declared at that time. General Musa, then commander-in-chief of the Pakistan forces, rightly claimed after the war that the Indian Air Force was not able to detect the Pattons even though they were moved in the daytime.

On the performance of the armoured division, Harbaksh Singh said in his report to the government:

> The action at Phillaur, it was claimed, surpassed even the sensational feats of Rommel at the height of his glory. The encounter between 6 Armoured Division and our 1 Armoured Division was euphemistically described as the Waterloo of the Patton tanks. The public caught in this mania of the prevailing self-adulation lapped up with smug satisfaction the inflated figures of enemy casualties in armour. This was all

very complimentary and it was also natural that in the first flush of victory India should be carried away by sentiments in which cold logic found no place. In fact, an objective assessment at that stage would have been frowned upon as unpatriotic. So we did a lot of mutual back-thumping. But when the dust settled down and the achievements of 1 Corps were viewed in their correct perspective, stripped of the aura of sensation, the initial feeling of exaltation gradually gave way to one of disillusionment. For, with the exception of a few major successes, the formation's record of operational performance was virtually a catalogue of lost chances. True, India dealt a telling blow to Pakistan but India conceded that it fell far short of a decisive defeat when it had the capacity to do so. In consequence, the enemy armour was only mauled, not destroyed.

11

Inquiries and Disclosures

'THE QUESTION IS MORAL, NOT LEGAL,' SAID MAHATMA GANDHI
when a Punjab Congress leader, Sardul Singh Kaeshwar, argued
that he was not legally bound to return a sum of Rs 500 since
the loan was time-barred. He was being considered for
membership to the Congress Working Committee. His name
was dropped, even though he eventually returned the money.
After Independence, the leaders of the freedom struggle were
keen on setting high standards in public life. They weighed
things on the scales of morality, not technicalities.

Jawaharlal Nehru made K.D. Malaviya, then the
petroleum minister, resign from cabinet because he could
not account for the contribution he had received for Congress
election funds from a businessman.

The pressure of public opinion worked. Malaviya had to
his credit the oil exploration in the country. Nehru had simply
accepted Lord Mountbatten's claim, based on his research in
London, that India had no oil and should not waste money in
exploring for it. It was Malaviya who had gone to Moscow,
and given India Bombay High. Nehru did not drive Malaviya
out of the Congress but did not give him any other assignment
all his life.

Again, Nehru bowed to public pressure when his favourite, Punjab chief minister Pratap Singh Kairon, was relentlessly attacked for his family's corruption. He had to appoint a Commission to look into the allegations against Kairon when the demand was made in the Lok Sabha. Nehru died before the Commission submitted its report.

I was in UNI when the then prime minister Lal Bahadur Shastri received the report in 1964. I knew S.R. Das, former chief justice of India, who headed the one-man Commission. He stayed in Delhi with his son-in-law, the then law minister, Ashok Sen. A few days after the submission of the report, I went to meet Das to get information on it. He thought I had to come to call on him. I too acted as if it was a casual visit. His talk was confined to pleasantries while I was waiting for an opportunity to mention the inquiry report on Kairon.

Finally, I told him that he looked like a student who had just finished an exam. I thought he would say something in reply. The report had taken the load off his shoulders, I repeated. He heaved a sigh of relief but kept quiet. I could see that he was relaxed because he was in his *banian* (vest) and had hung up his shirt on a peg in the wall. It took me some time before I could bring him to talk of Kairon's corruption.

Did he write the report in hand I asked. He replied in the affirmative.

I had heard that he wrote out his judgements in hand when he was at the Bench. Writing a hundred pages by hand must have been tiring, I prodded. No, it was a short report, less than twenty-five pages, he said. I was happy with this exchange because I had gathered two pieces of information: that the report was handwritten and that it was limited to twenty-five pages. All this would give body to my story. But the sixty-four thousand dollar question still remained to be answered: Had the report found Kairon guilty or not?

I tried to engage Das on all types of topics but he was not forthcoming. His replies were monosyllabic, as if he did not want to talk. On how many charges did you find him guilty, I asked. He did not say anything in reply except that the number did not matter. This gave me an inkling that some charges against Kairon had stuck, but not many. I thought I would ask him a direct question. Did any allegation implicate Kairon?

He was somewhat taken aback by my approach but remained calm. I could see that he was embarrassed. He looked at me in a way that signified that the conversation was over. I had to get up, albeit reluctantly. While bidding him goodbye, I said the government would not like the report. This was a googly of sorts. He was clean-bowled. The reply gave him away. He said a judge had to do an unpleasant job, whether it found favour with the government or not. He said he was sorry if the government did not like his job.

I was now certain that Kairon had been found guilty. I returned to the office and wrote that Pratap Singh Kairon had been found guilty by the Das Commission in the twenty-five page report it had submitted to the government, and that the judge had written the report in his own hand. As it turned out the Commission had exonerated Kairon on all counts except one – the misuse of the civil surgeon at Jalandhar. The chief minister had taken him along on a visit to Kangra, now part of Himachal Pradesh.

Many newspapers, which bought the UNI service, front-paged the story. Shastri sent cabinet secretary Khera to Chandigarh, the headquarters of the Punjab government, to inform Kairon about the findings; the chief minister submitted his resignation to the state governor. Eminent cartoonist Rajinder Puri drew a cartoon for the *Hindustan Times*, showing a surprised Kairon saying that he had left the government on a UNI report, not on Das's. Nehru would not have asked Kairon to quit for such a minor indiscretion. But Shastri had never liked Kairon and often described him as 'Panditji's weakness'. Like Morarji Desai, who believed all his life that I was responsible for installing Shastri as the prime minister after Nehru's death, Kairon never forgave me.

Incidentally, Desai and Kairon were close friends.

~

My disclosure of Justice H.R. Khanna's inquiry report on allegations against Biju Patnaik, former Orissa chief minister, was equally upsetting and drew wide attention.

The probe covered the period when he occupied office. Shastri appointed a Committee of three cabinet ministers, T.T. Krishnamachari, M.C. Chagla and Ashok Sen, to examine the inquiry report and recommend action, if any, to the government. The press would report daily that the Committee had met but disclosed nothing about what Justice Khanna's report had found.

I went one evening to Ashok Sen, whom I knew intimately, and asked him if I could borrow the report for an hour, and sit in his side-room to go through it. To my surprise, he agreed to give me the report on the condition that I would return it the following morning. This was a big task because the report was voluminous.

Returning to the UNI office, I collected at one place all the teleprinter operators and reporters known for their typing speed. I untagged the report and distributed the pages among them. We worked through the night and made five copies of the report. The following morning, I returned the report to Sen. (Photocopying machines had not yet come to India; I am talking of a time as far back as forty years.)

Before releasing the story on the report, I met Patnaik at his residence on Aurengzeb Road in New Delhi. I told him that I wanted his version so that I could run both, the report and his defence. First, he would not believe that I had the report. Subsequently, he threatened to sue me and UNI for rupees one crore each. Then he offered to buy shares of UNI and also purchase the service for his daily paper, *Kalinga,* provided I did not use the story. It was a tempting offer because UNI was then a struggling news agency, not even earning enough to cover the salary bill. I told him that I would await his response for 24 hours. If I did not hear from him, I would run the story.

He did not send any word. I ran the story. Many papers used it on the front page.

True to his word, Biju sued me and UNI.

What could we do? Legal experts advised us to establish the authenticity of the report. This, they said, could be done if it was made public. One way they suggested was to place it on the table of any of the two Houses in Parliament. I entrusted this work to the bulky Joshi, the senior-most correspondent in UNI.

Our effort to place the report in the Rajya Sabha was foiled by the then chairman S. Radhakrishnan. He expressed his unhappiness over the attempt. Finally, Joshi was able to persuade the stormy petrel H.V. Kamath to place the report on the Lok Sabha table.

Kapur Singh was the speaker. He was not too happy with the ruling Congress and gave permission to Kamath to place the report on the table of the House. Suddenly it was all over.

Our rival news agency, PTI, had to run the report because it was a big disclosure. When the then home minister Gulzarilal Nanda was asked in parliament whether the report placed on the table was genuine, he said he could neither deny nor confirm it. This was quite an embarrassing moment for the government. Parliament was up in arms.

Prime Minister Lal Bahadur Shastri ordered a CBI inquiry into the matter...

12

Identifying the Source

S. KANDASWAMI, A TOP CBI OFFICIAL, WAS ENTRUSTED WITH the job of tracing the leak of Justice Khanna's report investigating allegations of corruption and misuse of power against former Orissa chief minister Biju Patnaik. Kandaswami rang me up early in the morning to find out whether I, as the head of UNI, knew who had done the story.

Kandaswami and I had worked together in the Home Ministry when Shastri was the home minister and we had been in touch off and on. What else could I say except that I would look into the matter? He never came back to me; he discovered immediately that I was the guilty party. I could not hide my name because the agency carried the initials of the reporter at the end of the copy. However, I alone could not take credit for the scoop. So many were involved in typing the report overnight and finding an MP in the Lok Sabha and his counterpart in the Rajya Sabha who would place the report on the table of the House. In any case, we had unanimously decided to stay mum.

Some UNI reporters informed me that the CBI had talked to them. Kandaswami wanted to find out who from the ministerial Committee, comprising three union ministers, had leaked the report. He asked many but drew a blank. Talking to UNI reporters or others in the media was of no use because I had not shared the source with anyone. Kandaswami spent a lot of time with all those who had worked with Justice Khanna.

Many in the Home Ministry who had processed the report were interrogated. I was relieved when I found that he was nowhere near the source.

Just when I thought the dust had settled, I got a frantic call from Law Minister Ashok Sen. I rushed to his house; he told me that the prime minister had asked all three members of the Committee to send him their copy of the report. Sen said that he had discovered to his horror that his copy was crumpled and stained. This was true because the copy Sen had given me had to be copied overnight. There was no way I could have done so without distributing the pages among several reporters and teleprinter operators for typing. There were bound to be fingerprints and other smudges on it because it was a hurried job. Sen showed me his copy. I requested him to delay its return as long as he could. He agreed but wondered what I would do in the meantime.

On my return to the office, I collected the senior staff and told them what had transpired between the law minister and myself. The only way I could think of was to smudge the other two copies, those of TTK (T.T. Krishnamachari, the then finance minister) and M.C. Chagla who, alongwith Sen, constituted the Committee.

Everyone in the staff thought that Chagla would be too solid a wall to breach. The former chief justice of India was reputed to be a man of principles. His legal training had made him impervious to journalistic ventures.

We considered TTK, a politician, more pliable and probably the weakest link. There were some reporters who knew him. One of them, who covered TTK's Ministry of Finance, was in contact with him practically every day. We expected him to get us TTK's copy. But the following day he informed me that TTK had refused and had expressed shock at the request. We were really in a soup but more so was our source, Ashok Sen. I did not know what to do.

Then one of the reporters told me that he knew TTK's personal assistant (PA). Both of them hailed from the same village. He approached him and found him willing to help. He promised to give us the copy of the report during the lunch hour when TTK would be away from office. We could have it then. This again would have to be a hurried job. The correspondent collected the copy a couple of days later. This time our problem was how to make the many-page report dirty in an hour's time. Once again the copy was unstapled. Its pages were distributed among the staff members. They were told to liberally smudge it with their fingers, crush it beneath their feet and do whatever they could think of to make the copy dirty. At last, TTK's copy was marked with several streaks. I thought we had done a fairly good job within the time at our disposal. The report was returned to TTK's house, a few minutes before the lunch break was over.

When the three reports were returned to Shastri, he examined them closely. He found two of them dirty. He sent for me and asked who from among the three ministers had given me the copy. I told him that the general impression was that he had done so since I had worked with him as information officer. Shastri smiled. He did not take time to guess who my source was as he knew of my connection with Sen. Shastri said that I had obtained the copy from Ashok Sen. I denied it. But my reply was not a straight yes or no. I told him that I had never met Kamath who had tabled the report in the Lok Sabha. If he were to recognize me I would accept any punishment the PM would propose.

Indeed, H.V. Kamath and I had never met before; Joshi, a senior UNI reporter, had given him the report. Shastri said he would follow my suggestion.

A few days later he held an identification parade at his house and made me stand in a line with some other people. Kamath was called in to identify me. He told Shastri that he had never seen me before. After some time, Shastri introduced me to Kamath.

Once it was established that I had not approached Kamath to table the report, Shastri called off the exercise. In any case, he knew who was responsible for the leakage and told me so. Had he pursued the matter to its logical end he would have had to ask Sen to resign from the government. This would have probably amounted to making a mountain out of a molehill.

Many people believed that I had got the report from Shastri since the responsibility for the leakage was not put on any minister. Shastri preferred that suspicion to the reshuffling of the cabinet.

Before leaving for Tashkent, where he died of a heart attack, Shastri got rid of Finance Minister T.T. Krishnamachari. The latter had to resign. No reasons were given but Shastri believed that he was 'mixed up' with certain elements that were 'not clean'. However, TTK told me: 'I could have stayed back if I had agreed to move from Finance.' He had opposed the devaluation of the rupee to which Shastri had agreed 'under pressure from America', as TTK put it.

According to him, 'The US won over Shastri by promising him an aid package of Rs 4000 crore.' It was not the first time that TTK was leaving the cabinet.

Several years earlier, he had resigned following certain Life Insurance Corporation transactions. At that time, Jawaharlal Nehru had told his colleagues that TTK had to leave because 'the minister must shoulder the responsibility for any decision or action of his secretary'. Nehru had written to the chief ministers then to praise TTK's 'great ability and perseverance' adding, 'his leaving us has been a great blow to me and to our government'.

After TTK's resignation, Indira Gandhi, who was the information minister, observed that it was only a matter of time before she would be crowded out under US pressure. According to Dinesh Singh, who was very close to Mrs Gandhi in those days, she even talked in terms of settling down in the UK and inquired about the cost of living there – She thought she could live off the royalties from her father's books!

13

The Tashkent Treaty

HAJI PIR AND TITHWAL IN KASHMIR WERE THE TWO POSTS which New Delhi recaptured during the 1965 war against Pakistan, on the logic that the entire Jammu and Kashmir state was India's. Prime Minister Lal Bahadur Shastri took the editors of the Indian news dailies into confidence, telling them that his government had decided not to vacate the posts. This was before he left for Tashkent in January 1966 to meet the Pakistan president General Mohammad Ayub Khan. The editors lapped up every word Shastri spoke – even when he said that he had first refused to go to Tashkent, but when Soviet prime minister Alexei Kosygin requested him a second time, he could not refuse because 'they have been consistent supporters of ours on Kashmir'.

Shastri wanted a large press contingent to accompany him to Tashkent because he wanted full coverage of his talks with Pakistan after 'winning the 1965 war'. It was a PR effort. Two planes flew to Tashkent via Teheran because Pakistan had stopped India's overflights after the war. Ironically, both Indian and Pakistani journalists were accommodated in the same hotel, at Hotel Tashkent; the latter, one storey below their Indian counterparts, on a separate floor.

On the very first day (3 January, 1966) the Indian officials told us that the Soviet Union was opposed to our retaining Haji Pir and Tithwal. While it favoured the proposal that Pakistan withdraw its 'armed personnel', including infiltrators, from Indian territory, Moscow felt that the liquidation of infiltrators was New Delhi's responsibility, and not Islamabad's.

From the first day it was clear that Pakistan's aim was to revive the question of Kashmir and India's to avoid it. In his inaugural speech, General Ayub Khan said that he would sign a no-war pact with India once 'the basic problem', meaning Kashmir, was resolved. Shastri emphasized that a no-war pact would help 'improve the totality of relations between India and Pakistan' because all the violence had spoilt the atmosphere.

Before the conference, Ayub told Kosygin, who was in close contact with the two sides, that he would not sign a no-war pact unless Shastri made 'some concession' on Kashmir. Ayub's information secretary, Altaf Gauhar, made it plain at his first press briefing in which Indian journalists were welcome – that without a solution on Kashmir 'a meaningful framework' between the countries was not possible.

Foreign Minister Zulfikar Ali Bhutto was in a sour mood from the start. All the Pakistani delegates had greeted Shastri's inaugural speech with loud cheers. Bhutto, however, sat impassively with his arms crossed. Later, after the speeches, when Ayub at the instance of Shastri, walked into a private room reserved for discussions, Bhutto wanted to join them. Ayub gestured his refusal; Bhutto was visibly angry.

The meeting was brief. Ayub suggested a formal agenda for the talks. Shastri did not think it necessary because he could foresee that it would mean a discussion on Kashmir – something he did not want to do. Yet, Kosygin was able to persuade him to talk on Kashmir by arguing that Ayub too had to cater to and mollify opinion in Pakistan.

Shastri agreed and, in a quid pro quo, Ayub conceded a discussion on ways to eschew violence. Obviously, Kosygin had done some arm-twisting to arrange this. Shastri was upset with me for having reported this on behalf of UNI, the news agency for which I worked now.

Shastri told Ayub that India would withdraw from Haji Pir and Tithwal provided Pakistan vacated Chhamb. Ayub's reply was that his forces would leave Chhamb if Indian forces withdrew from all Pakistani areas, including Sind. Shastri pointed out that Chhamb was in Jammu and Kashmir and so were Haji Pir and Tithwal, therefore they should be taken up together; the rest should be dealt with separately.

Ayub stuck to his demand that both sides should withdraw from all territories they had occupied during the conflict. Ironically, however divergent in their views, both leaders conducted their conversation in Hindustani, a mixture of Urdu and Hindi, and the language spoken in India and Pakistan. They could not help it; both were more at ease with Hindustani, even though they had begun the talks in English.

Shastri told Ayub, and later Kosygin, that India was willing to withdraw from all territories if Pakistan agreed to sign a no-war pact. Ayub said he would consider the suggestion. Shastri's effort was to ensure that Pakistan would abjure violence to settle Kashmir and other issues with India.

Meanwhile, the talks on the preparation of agenda at the ministerial level between Foreign Minister Swaran Singh (who had accompanied Shastri) and Bhutto, got embroiled in a discussion on Kashmir. Bhutto insisted on its inclusion on the plea that no peace between India and Pakistan was possible until the Kashmir issue was settled. Swaran Singh said that the sovereignty of India over the state was not a matter open to discussion. Swaran Singh expressed his willingness to discuss other matters but Bhutto thought they were 'peripheral'. India's stance was that, by solving other problems first, there would be enough goodwill generated to make it easier to tackle the issue of Kashmir.

New Delhi was convinced in its own mind – and Nehru once wrote to President Kennedy saying as much – that Kashmir was a symptom, not the disease, of Indo–Pakistan estrangement. Even if Kashmir was presented to Pakistan on a platter, the relations between the two countries would not improve because the very existence of Pakistan was dependent on anti-Indian feelings.

As 'another matter', Bhutto mentioned the 'ousting of Muslims' from Assam and West Bengal. In the Fifties, India discovered that Muslims from East Pakistan had surreptitiously entered Assam (2,50,000) and West Bengal (1,16,000), apparently for economic reasons. New Delhi then began checking the extent of infiltration and sending back 'non-citizens'. Between 1961 and 1967 as many as 1,79,258 infiltrators were sent back from Assam and 16,381 from West Bengal. Many genuine Indians were also thrown out in the process and ultimately the government set up special courts to listen to appeals against 'quit orders'. Swaran Singh readily agreed to bring up these subjects for discussion between the home ministers of the two countries.

However, the deadlock between Shastri and Ayub did not end. Kosygin shuttled between the two camps and persuaded them to meet for a 'final' session. If at all he was successful in anything it was merely this: At the meeting between the two, Ayub produced a four-line draft which he hoped would satisfy Shastri on the question of the renunciation of force. The draft contained only a general statement on the efficacy of finding a solution to Indo–Pakistan problems through peace. Shastri was not satisfied and proposed an amendment which Ayub accepted. In his own hand, the Pakistan president made the necessary change in the draft, including the phrase, 'without resort to arms'. (Our Ministry of External Affairs has the document in its archives.)

When India asked for an official confirmation of the amended draft, Pakistan said that no such draft existed. Bhutto, apparently, had had his way by threatening to go back to Pakistan straightaway and 'taking the nation into confidence'; telling it how Ayub buckled under Shastri's threats because he could not take chances; he had emerged weaker from the 1965 conflict.

It was not Ayub but Bhutto who rang up Shastri's dacha to explain that Ayub had agreed to put in the phrase 'without resort to arms' on the promise of Indian 'concessions' on Kashmir. Now even Shastri began telling the members of his delegation that they should get ready to return to India. An innocuous kind of statement, saying that further efforts would be made to solve Indo–Pakistan differences, was prepared.

When Ayub's retraction reached Shastri's camp, Andrei Gromyko, the Soviet foreign minister at the time, was with the Indian delegation. Bhutto called Gromyko to inform him of Ayub's reply and Gromyko admonished Bhutto in their presence. Bhutto said that when Ayub had agreed to renounce the use of force, India had promised to show some concession on Kashmir. Gromyko said, 'That is a lie.'

The Tashkent meet was practically over, much to the regret of the Soviet leaders. The Indian spokesman continued to hedge and prevaricate, claiming that the talks had reached 'a delicate stage'. But the Pakistani delegates were quite outspoken and said that they were packing their bags to go home. The Pakistani journalists said that their bags were already being loaded.

Kosygin told Shastri that the UN Charter enjoined upon all the members to use peaceful methods and that he should not specifically ask for the renunciation of force. 'Then you will have to talk to some other Indian prime minister,' Shastri said. Kosygin hastily withdrew his observation saying: 'This is what Ayub said.' Kosygin then took a different tack and asked Shastri to show some 'concession' on Kashmir. Shastri did not agree – not even to a statement that he and Ayub would meet later to discuss Kashmir.

It was Kosygin who saved the situation. He used all his persuasive power – as well as some pressure – to make Shastri not insist on a specific reference to renunciation of force in the proposed peace agreement.

On his part, the Soviet leader gave an assurance that his country would support India if ever Pakistan tried to take Kashmir by force. Kosygin also worked on Ayub to agree to the pledge of renunciation of force indirectly by reaffirming in the proposed agreement under the UN Charter that the parties concerned were obliged to adopt peaceful means to settle differences.

The Pakistan president also conceded the point that the armed personnel would withdraw to the positions they had held on 5 August 1965 – the day on which Pakistani infiltrators first started entering Kashmir. Shastri, who earlier was not even willing to accept the mention of Kashmir in the proposed agreement, also made a gesture by conceding to the mention of the fact that Kashmir was discussed, with each side setting forth its respective position.

India had to vacate Haji Pir and Tithwal. Later, Shastri confided in Indian journalists that in the face of Kosygin's stand, the Security Council would have gone to the extent of imposing sanctions against India if it had not withdrawn its forces from the two posts. 'I didn't have much choice,' he said.

14

Death in Tashkent

I WAS INDIA'S HIGH COMMISSIONER IN LONDON IN 1990 WHEN a busybody from Moscow met me to ask if he could get a free air ticket to Delhi. Checking up on him I found that he was an academician who travelled back and forth on New Delhi's hospitality. I was more interested in learning whether the papers, which had been made public by Moscow after the disintegration of the Soviet Union, had anything on Shastri's death in Tashkent. 'I have seen all the papers but there was nothing on Shastri's death,' he said. I found this difficult to believe. The man got up abruptly and said he would come again; he never did although I stayed in London for another five months after the meeting.

This incident somewhat confirmed my earlier suspicion that there was more to Shastri's death than what I knew. The belief took a deeper hold of me when Foreign Secretary T.N. Kaul rang me one day when I was resident editor of the *Statesman* in Delhi. He had been India's ambassador to Moscow when Shastri died on 11 January 1966. He requested me to issue a statement saying that Shastri had died of a heart attack. A Lok Sabha member, Dharm Yash Dev, had alleged in the House that Shastri had been poisoned. His charge was that

Shastri used to get his meals from Kaul's residence in Tashkent and that he was given poison in the food he ate after signing the Tashkent Agreement. Kaul was close to the Nehru family, especially Mrs Indira Gandhi who succeeded Shastri.

Kaul told me on the phone: 'One word from you will end the doubt because you were very close to Shastri.' He sounded extremely worried and begged me to say that it was a heart attack. Till then, not even an iota of doubt had crossed my mind, and I still believe that Shastri died of a heart attack.

I do, however, recall every bit of what happened on that day.

The breakthrough in the talks between India and Pakistan at Tashkent happened around noon. Shastri addressed the Indian journalists soon after. They were not happy that India had to part with Haji Pir and Tithwal, the two posts, in the face of Shastri's avowal not to return them. A few of them were even aggressive. I felt that our job was to report, not to hold an inquisition, which, to my mind, was what three or four journalists from leading English newspapers were unashamedly doing. The prime minister sat impassively. He finally said in an almost imploring tone: 'I am in your hands. Everything depends on how you convey the news of this Agreement to the country.' A couple of journalists continued to badger him. He explained that he had been left with no choice when Prime Minister Kosygin threatened to side with Pakistan.

Kaul hosted a reception that afternoon. I went up to Shastri to assure him that most journalists had sent favourable dispatches. He was quite convinced that he had opened a new chapter of peace and conciliation with Pakistan and talked to me in that vein for a while. Then he suddenly changed his tone to tell me that General Ayub Khan had invited him to tea the following day in Islamabad. The original plans were to stop first in Kabul to meet Khan Abdul Ghaffar Khan who wanted an independent Pakhtoonistan carved out of Pakistan.

Really speaking, we should not have been stopping in Kabul at all, Shastri said, because that would mean violating the spirit of the Tashkent Agreement.

In the evening the Soviet Government threw a lavish party at Hotel Tashkent. Whisky and vodka flowed like water and the tables were choked with food. I stayed for half an hour but preferred to retire since the plane to Kabul was to leave early. I was already dozing when someone pounded on my door. I thought I was having a bad dream. I heard someone saying, 'Your prime minister is dying!' in English with a Russian accent. Then I saw myself in a big crowd gathered around Shastri's dead body.

When I reached the distant dacha where Shastri was staying, Kosygin and a couple of Soviet officers were standing in the veranda. They gestured with their hands to say that Shastri was no more. The doctors who had been attending to Shastri were still sitting in the drawing room, and I could see Shastri lying still and inert, through the open door. I went into the room. The big bed and the spacious room with its high ceiling made Shastri look even smaller than he was; a dot in a large expanse. His slippers were neatly placed beside his bed. Far in the corner, on a dressing table, lay an overturned thermos bottle, speaking volumes about the effort he must have made to get a drink of water. There was no buzzer or bell in his room with which he could have summoned help. His private assistant's room was about fifteen yards away. One had to walk through an open corridor to reach it. His sitting room had three telephones: one local, one trunk and one connected with his PAs', who also had the extensions of the local and trunk telephones. Another Indian journalist and I searched the dacha for the national flag and flowers. We found them and covered Shastri's body with them because soon the entire world would be beating at the dacha's windows to pay homage to India's prime minister.

From information pieced together from Shastri's personal staff I gathered that the prime minister, after attending the farewell reception, had reached his dacha around 10 p.m. Sahay, Sharma and Ram Nath – all on Shastri's personal staff – trooped into his room. They had heard about Ayub's invitation to tea at Islamabad. Loyal and devoted as they were, they wanted him not to fly over Pakistan because they feared that the Pakistanis 'could do any mischief'. Sharma recalled how the Gujarat chief minister, Balwant Rai Mehta, had been killed during the India–Pakistan conflict when a Pakistani plane had downed his Dakota. Shastri had assured them: 'Now we have an Agreement. Moreover, Ayub is a nice person.' He told Ram Nath to bring him his food which was prepared in the dacha by the Russians.

The kitchen had a Soviet cook who was helped by two ladies, both from the Russian Intelligence Department, and they tasted everything, including the water, before it was served to Shastri. John Mohammed, Kaul's cook, was also a helper, mostly used by Shastri's personal staff to prepare non-vegetarian dishes. At times, he prepared special food for Shastri at Kaul's house.

Shastri's frugal vegetarian meal on the night of his death consisted of sag and alu (spinach and potatoes) and a curry. Since he had eaten at the farewell party, he partook very little of these. While he was eating, a call came through from Delhi. Sahay took the call, which was from Venkatraman, another of Shastri's personal assistants. He told Sahay that the reaction in Delhi to the Tashkent Declaration was favourable but that the household was not happy. He said that Surendra Nath Dwivedi, the PSP (Praja Socialist Party) leader and Atal Behari Vajpayee, the Jana Sangh leader, had criticized the withdrawal of Indian forces from Haji Pir and Tithwal. When Shastri was told about this, he said that it was a given thing that the Opposition would criticize the Agreement.

Sahay asked Shastri if he should connect him to the house. He had not talked to his family in two days. Shastri first said no but then changed his mind. Sahay got through to Shastri's house in New Delhi in no time. It was around 11 p.m. Tashkent time (which was half an hour behind Indian time). First, his younger son-in-law, V.N. Singh, spoke, but he did not say much. Then Kusam, Shastri's eldest and favourite daughter, took over the phone. Shastri asked her in Hindi: *'Tujhe kaisa laga?'* (How did you react to it?) She replied: *'Babuji, hamein achha nahin laga.'* (I have not liked it.) He asked, 'What about Amma?' referring to his wife. She too had not liked it, was Kusam's reply. Shastri observed: *'Agar gharwalon ko achha nahin laga, to bahar wale kya kahengay?* (If it has not been liked by the family, what will outsiders say?)

Shastri then asked his daughter to give the telephone to Mrs Shastri. Kusam replied that Amma did not want to talk to him because she was angry over the return of Hajipur and Tithwal to Islamabad. Despite Shastri's many requests, Mrs Shastri did not come to the phone. Shastri then asked for the morning newspapers to be sent to Kabul where an Indian Air Force plane was reaching the next day to fly him back to Delhi.

The telephone conversation, according to Sahay, appeared to have upset Shastri. He paced up and down his room. This was not unusual. Even during interviews, he would often do this while he spoke. But that night it was almost an unending walk in the room. For a person who had had two heart attacks earlier, the telephone conversation and the walking must have been a strain.

Ramnath gave Shastri a glass of milk, which he used to drink before he retired every night. The prime minister again started walking up and down and later asked for water which was given from the thermos flask on the dressing table. It was a little after midnight when Shastri told Ramnath to go to his room and get some sleep because he had to get up early to leave for Kabul the next day. Ramnath offered to sleep on the floor in Shastri's room but he was asked to go to his own room upstairs.

Sahay recalled later that the PAs had finished packing the luggage at 1.20 a.m. Tashkent time. They were still talking when they saw Shastri at the door. With great difficulty, Shastri asked: 'Where is doctor sahib?'

Shastri's physician, Dr Chug, was sleeping in the room in which the PAs were packing the luggage. Sahay shouted for Chug, while Sharma, assisted by the Indian security-man, helped Shastri to walk back to his room. If it was a heart attack – a myocardiac infarction, an obstruction of blood supply to the heart muscles – as the Soviet doctors observed later, this walk, even though he was being assisted, must have been fatal.

It was in the sitting room that Shastri had a coughing bout that would not cease. His personal assistants helped him to bed. Sharma gave him water and remarked: 'Babuji, now you will be all right.' Shastri just touched his hand to his chest and fell unconscious. Later, when Mrs Shastri was told by Sharma in Delhi that he had given Shastri water she said: 'You are a very lucky person because you gave him the last cup of water.'

Dr Chug felt Shastri's pulse and tearfully said: 'Babuji, you did not give me time.' He gave him an injection in the arm and later injected him directly in the heart. Finding no response, he attempted mouth-to-mouth resuscitation.

Chug asked Sahay to get the Russian doctors. The Soviet Government had posted a security-man who, on hearing the word 'doctor' from Sahay, ran for help. A lady doctor arrived ten minutes later, followed by some more doctors. They found Shastri dead. The death was at 1.32 a.m. Tashkent time.

General Ayub Khan was genuinely grieved by Shastri's death. He came to Shastri's dacha at about 4 a.m., and looking at his body, said that he was a man of peace who had given his life for amity between India and Pakistan. Later, Ayub told Pakistani journalists that Shastri was one man with whom he had hit it off; Pakistan and India might have sorted out their problems if he had lived, he said.

When I returned from Tashkent, Mrs Shastri asked me why Shastri's body had turned blue. I replied: 'When bodies are embalmed I am told they turn blue.' She then inquired about 'certain cuts' on Shastri's body. I said I knew nothing about them; I had not seen the body.

Apparently, she and the others in the family suspected foul play. A few days later I heard that Mrs Shastri was angry with some of the personal assistants who accompanied Shastri because they had refused to sign a statement alleging that Shastri did not die a natural death.

As the days went by, the Shastri family grew more convinced that Shastri had been poisoned. In 1970, on 2 October, Shastri's birthday, Mrs Shastri openly asked for an official investigation into her husband's death. The family was upset that John Mohammed, Kaul's cook, had been allowed to assist Ram Nath in the kitchen in Tashkent. This was a silly allegation because John Mohammed had also prepared food for Shastri when he had visited Moscow in 1965, before the Tashkent Agreement.

Following rumours of an unnatural death, the Congress party Old Guard supported the demand for a probe into Shastri's death. I asked Morarji Desai towards the end of October 1970 whether he really believed that Shastri had not died a natural death. Desai said: 'This is all politics. I am sure there was no foul play. He died of a heart attack. I have checked with the doctor and his secretary, C.P. Srivastava, who accompanied him to Tashkent.'

15

Shastri's Successors

LAL BAHADUR SHASTRI'S DEATH IN TASHKENT ON 11 JANUARY 1966, was an unexpected blow. Home Minister Gulzarilal Nanda was made the officiating prime minister. But this time Morarji Desai, waiting in the wings, was a serious contestant. Information Minister Indira Gandhi, who kept her own counsel, was another. Yet another candidate, Defence Minister Yeswantrao Balwantarao Chavan, was travelling with Shastri's body to New Delhi. Once again, it fell upon Congress president K. Kamaraj to decide who should succeed Shastri. Kamaraj reiterated the formula laid down after Nehru's death: that the Congress high command would decide how to go about it. The party's Parliamentary Party would follow the line indicated.

Who would the next prime minister be, I wondered? Shastri had once told me his view while recovering from a mild heart attack he had had within a few days of becoming prime minister. If he were to die within a year or so, he said, Indira Gandhi would be the prime minister, but if he lived for three or four years, Chavan would be the one. I told this to Chavan and Swaran Singh in Tashkent after Shastri's death. Chavan wanted me to write about it. Several years later, when I checked with Kamaraj, he said Shastri's assessment had been correct.

Kamaraj flew in a special plane to Delhi. R. Venkataraman, who later became India's president, accompanied him. He was Kamaraj's confidant. After telling Venkataraman that Indira Gandhi was the only alternative, he went to sleep. An hour before the plane landed he woke up to repeat to Venkataraman that the Congress had no option except Indira Gandhi. She was the only one who could steer the party to victory in the next Lok Sabha election – due a year later (1967). Kamaraj had another reason to choose Indira Gandhi. He had asked Nehru during his illness whether Indira Gandhi should occupy the position of prime minister. Nehru, according to Kamaraj, did not rule out the proposition but indicated that it should be Lal Bahadur first and then Indu. Since this coversation between Kamaraj and myself took place during the Emergency, he used the opportunity to curse himself for making this choice: She was the best the Congress leaders had to offer, he said. Gulzarilal Nanda, in his eyes, was a confused person who could not be trusted with India's leadership. He continued to see in Morarji Desai a person who would only talk about Hindi and the north – the two things he feared would tell upon India's homogeneity. Kamaraj also knew that he could not stop Morarji from contesting the leadership this time.

Kamaraj did not know fully about Indira Gandhi's attitude towards Shastri. When Shastri was minister without portfolio, Indira Gandhi treated him shabbily. When Nehru was sick, lying in bed in the room upstairs, she made Shastri wait for one hour before allowing him to meet Nehru. A successor to Nehru deserved better treatment. But Nehru had no way of knowing how Indira Gandhi abused authority in his name. As the days went by, Shastri felt more and more exasperated. In fact, he had to wait even to get an appointment with Nehru. He even considered quitting the Ministry. Once he told me that he would go back to Allahabad: 'There is nothing for me here now,' he had said. He then added woefully: 'If I continue to stay in Delhi I am bound to have a clash with Panditji because he has allowed Indiraji to rule in his name. I would rather retire from politics than join issue with him.'

Two considerations made him stay. One, the Old Guard, (also known as the Syndicate), did not want him to give up the position of vantage he occupied as cabinet minister, even though he was ranked number 4.

Two, by quitting, Shastri feared he would destroy the impression that Nehru had nominated him his successor when he had brought him back into the government.

Many Congress leaders at that time said – and told him so – that Nehru's 'coolness' towards Shastri was influenced by Indira Gandhi's 'hostility' towards him. Initially, Shastri did not encourage such talk but later he went out of his way to find out if what people said was true. In due course he was convinced that he was not uppermost in Nehru's mind as his successor. There was somebody else. I, his press secretary, ventured to ask Shastri at that time: 'Who do you think Nehru has in mind as his successor?' Shastri said that he had his daughter in mind

'But it won't be easy,' I told him. 'The general impression is that you are such a staunch devotee of Nehru that you would yourself propose Indira Gandhi's name after his death.'

'I am not as much of a sadhu as you imagine me to be,' was Shastri's reply.

There is no doubt that Nehru had his daughter in mind. Once, when Dhebar Bhai, the Congress president, was to step down, the party's Working Committee discussed many names. Someone mentioned Indira Gandhi. Gobind Ballabh Pant, then the home minister, intervened to say that her health was not good. It was a fatherly comment made because he had seen her growing up in Allahabad. Nehru intervened angrily, saying: 'She is stronger than all of us. She is not ill in any way.'

After Nehru's outburst, Indira Gandhi was unanimously elected the Congress president.

Atulya Ghosh, a top Congress leader from West Bengal, was the first to meet Kamaraj on his arrival in Delhi and conveyed to him the decision reached by the Old Guard to put him up as a candidate. Kamaraj was not prepared to listen. He admonished Ghosh for creating 'problems' instead of helping him.

Kamaraj knew his limitations. He told me once: 'I could have probably become the prime minister but I did not think it fair or proper because I did not know either Hindi or English; the knowledge of at least one is essential for India's prime minister.'

However, M. Bhaktavatsalam, who was his associate for many years in Tamil Nadu and who succeeded him as its chief minister, told me something else: 'What deterred Kamaraj was the possibility of a contest. He (Kamaraj) knew that a person from the south could not defeat Morarji from north India; Mrs Gandhi could because she hailed from Uttar Pradesh.' Kamaraj worked hard to make the Syndicate support Indira Gandhi. When Karnataka chief minister S. Nijalingappa and S.K. Patil, a strongman from Maharashtra, warned him that she would one day turn against them all, he laughed at the observation. He said he knew her better. 'I was proved wrong; she wanted all the power for herself and allowed nobody to come anywhere near her,' Kamaraj admitted later.

Once the juggernaut of the Syndicate rolled in Indira Gandhi's favour, it was clear who would win. There was a mad scramble to jump onto her bandwagon, with the chief ministers taking the lead. Y.B. Chavan and Gulzarilal Nanda withdrew, but not Morarji, who fought till the end. For the first time in the history of the Congress Parliamentary Party, there was a contest for leadership.

Mrs Gandhi secured 355 votes and Morarji Desai less than half that number, 169.

There was no doubting the popularity of the party choice. For most people it marked the continuation of the Nehru legend that had been briefly interrupted by Shastri. The common man was happy at the thought that their hero's daughter (Nehru's *bitiya*) was at the helm of affairs.

The reaction of political parties was on predictable lines. The right suspected her of harbouring communist leanings – the Jana Sangh and the Swatantra parties said openly that she was pro-Soviet. To the left, she was more acceptable than Morarji Desai. The communists had no option after Nanda's withdrawal, though they had many scores to settle with her. As the Congress party's president she had been uncompromising towards them. She was the one who had forced Nehru to dismiss the communist government in Kerala on 31 July, 1959 even though it had a majority in the legislature. EMS Namboodiripad, the then chief minister, told me that Nehru expressed his 'unhappiness and helplessness' when he met him prior to his government's dismissal. When asked after the election if she was a representative of the left, Mrs Gandhi had replied: 'I am a representative of all India, which includes all shades of opinion.' But her position was soon clear. Where Shastri tended to tilt towards the right, her inclination was to the left. And she appeared determined to correct whatever deviations had taken place from Nehru's socialist policies. But her priority was to first broaden her own base and then her party's, in that order. She had elections in mind, and shared the thought with Kamaraj. But she did not show him her list of cabinet members before sending it to the president of India. The Congress president was always consulted on the formation of the cabinet.

Kamaraj regretted the decision to appoint Indira Gandhi. In a conversation with me during the Emergency, he went on cursing himself for having made Indira Gandhi the prime minister. His greatest regret was that during the Emergency (1975-77) she inducted Sanjay Gandhi, her son, as an extra-Constitutional authority.

Indira Gandhi's Reign

16

Indira Gandhi and the Old Guard

MY REQUEST FOR AN INTERVIEW WITH PRIME MINISTER INDIRA
Gandhi had been pending for a long time. One day in
December, nearly ten months after she came to power on
19 January 1966, there was a call from her office inviting me
to accompany her on a special air-force plane to Shantiniketan.
She would talk to me during the flight.

I could never have foreseen that my interview would
initiate the process that split the Congress three years later.

The party's president, K. Kamaraj, was instrumental in
installing Indira Gandhi as the prime minister. Now he was
the one who wanted to chastise her. He was angry that she
had devalued the rupee under US pressure. She, in turn, was
against him because she suspected that he and the rest of the
old leadership were trying to dictate to her. In reality, the
prime minister and the party president had drifted apart soon
after she had assumed power.

Since the differences between the two were no more a
secret, I asked her during the interview to define her equation
with Kamaraj. She did not reply to my question. Was the party
behind you? I persisted. She said in a shrill tone that everything
depended on 'whom people want and whom the party

wanted'. By then the general elections had been announced. Mrs Gandhi's reference was obvious. On my return, Kamaraj asked me if she had made the remark to differentiate between people and the party. I simply played back the tape-recording of our conversation as evidence.

Kamaraj's worry was that the public airing of differences between him and the prime minister would harm the Congress at the polls. Already the devaluation of the rupee and the consequent rise in prices had dented the party's popularity. Mrs Gandhi was also conscious that her hold on the party was limited.

The Old Guard, which came to be known as the 'Syndicate', was not happy with the increasing influence that 'the chit of a girl' – the term they used for her – had come to have. On the other hand, she found to her dismay that most of her supporters had been denied a Congress ticket.

It was evident that the party bosses were determined to weaken her standing. They were playing their same old game– selecting only those candidates for the Lok Sabha and state assembly elections who would do their bidding. Jawaharlal Nehru too, when he was the prime minister, had not been happy with this procedure for selecting suitable electoral candidates.

After Independence, soon after the first general elections, he unburdened himself in a letter to the country's ministers: 'Many who would have made excellent candidates have preferred not to stand at all because of the atmosphere of charge and counter-charge. Indeed, politics in India, as perhaps elsewhere, gradually tends to eliminate the sensitive person. Only the tough survive.'

Left to herself, Mrs Gandhi told me in the interview, she would have chosen 'some better candidates'. She said: 'Now the need is for specialized knowledge. I would not like only specialized people to be chosen but we should have a sprinkling of them to study particular subjects. There should be experts to raise the level of debate in parliament.'

This was only a pious statement. Some of the candidates she had recommended were not specialists. They were nameless people, with no merit. Their only qualification was that they were totally and blindly loyal to her personally. Nonetheless, she was right in claiming that her position in the country was 'uncontestable'. As Nehru's daughter, she was popular among the masses. Still, she did not take on the Old Guard. It was not that she lacked courage; it was her intuition which told her that the time had not yet come to challenge the party bosses.

The result of the general elections, the fourth since Independence, jolted the Congress. It secured only 281 seats, a working majority of 21 in the then 520-member Lok Sabha. The party had lost 83 seats in the House. Also, it barely managed to win half of the state assembly seats in the country: 1688 out of 3483.

The party lost its majority in eight states: Uttar Pradesh, Bihar, West Bengal, Orissa, Tamil Nadu, Kerala, Rajasthan and Punjab, and the two Union Territories of Delhi and Manipur. The Jana Sangh, openly advocating a Hindu Rashtriya against the country's secular ethos, made gains in Uttar Pradesh, Madhya Pradesh and Rajasthan, the Hindi-speaking states. The rightist Swatantra Party won in Gujarat and Orissa. The communists improved their position marginally in all the states except Andhra Pradesh and, surprisingly, West Bengal where there was a straight contest between the right and the left. The rout of the Congress was exemplary in Tamil Nadu; the appeal by the Dravida Munnetra Kazhagam (DMK) against 'north Indian chauvinism' brought about the debacle of the Congress, getting it only 49 out of 234 seats.

To Mrs Gandhi's relief, many Congress bosses among the Old Guard were defeated. Among them were Kamaraj and C. Subramaniam from Tamil Nadu, S.K. Patil from Maharashtra and Atulya Ghosh from West Bengal. A notable casualty in the opposition was former defence minister Krishna Menon who had contested from his old constituency in Bombay as an independent candidate after the Congress had refused him a ticket. In their post-election analysis, the party bosses came to the conclusion that their defeat was due to the government's 'poor' economic policies and still 'poorer implementation' of them. Kamaraj renewed the attack on devaluation. Mrs Gandhi's supporters, on the other hand, said that, but for her, the Congress would have fared even worse. A few of her associates alleged that Kamaraj had purposely fielded in the north only those candidates who would lose so that Mrs Gandhi's would fail to muster the necessary party parliamentary backing to be re-elected as prime minister.

After the polls, Morarji Desai again threw his hat into the ring, bidding for leadership. He was confident because this time Kamaraj was on his side. Undoubtedly, if Kamaraj had had his way, Morarji would have led the Congress in parliament. Morarji even told me that Kamaraj would have made him prime minister.

But what could they do? Despite the election results, the majority in the party was behind Mrs Gandhi. So were leaders like Y.B. Chavan, the Maharashtra boss with a solid block of votes. In an interview to me, before the elections, Chavan had announced his support for Mrs Gandhi. Still Morarji went down fighting and insisting on his 'legitimate right' to be prime minister – after having been blocked twice before. The Congress did not want any split in its ranks, particularly when it had only a small majority in the Lok Sabha.

Once again, Morarji lost. This time, his two supporters, Chief Minister Chandra Bhan Gupta from UP and Chief Minister Dwarka Prasad Mishra from Madhya Pradesh came to Delhi and made Morarji accept a compromise. He agreed to withdraw on the condition that he would be designated deputy prime minister. Mrs Gandhi accepted the proposal. After consolidating his position as the deputy prime minister, Morarji then pressed for the home portfolio. He wanted the same status that Sardar Patel had in Nehru's Cabinet. Mrs Gandhi refused. Her ardent supporter, Y.B. Chavan, was given the home portfolio instead. Morarji was given finance. It was another matter that two and half years later, she hounded him for that portfolio as well. The Old Guard felt relieved because Morarji, their candidate, was in the cabinet. Their satisfaction knew no bounds when Mrs Gandhi appointed Neelam Sanjeeva Reddy, their Man Friday, as the Lok Sabha speaker. She had dropped him from her cabinet earlier.

All Mrs Gandhi's moves, as those of the Old Guard, had long-term implications. Both knew that the fight for supremacy in the Congress was inevitable. Yet neither wanted to be seen as spoiling for a fight.

Both wanted to make sure that the Congress stayed in power. The Old Guard was against Mrs Gandhi, not against the party. Since differences between the two sides were increasing, a clash was bound to take place. The untimely death of Dr Zakir Hussain, the then president of India, provided them with an opportunity for a show of strength.

17

The Battle for President

ZAKIR HUSSAIN'S BODY HAD SCARCELY TURNED COLD WHEN the jockeying for his successor started in Rashtrapati Bhavan itself.

The embarrassing part was that the family of V.V. Giri – the then vice-president, who automatically became acting president – moved in, eyeing Rashtrapati Bhavan and selecting the room each one would occupy. There were four sons and their wives, seven daughters and their husbands, and thirty-nine grandchildren. Their wranglings on the one hand combined with that of the Congress leaders' over the successor on the other, made the otherwise solemn occasion a bit of a farce. The atmosphere invoked memories of the day when Jawaharlal Nehru's body lay at Teen Murti House. On that occasion, too, Congress leaders had been in a huddle, not far from the body, squabbling over, *After Nehru, Who?*

The Congress had not been so divided then as it was when Zakir Hussain died on 3 May 1969. The profound sense of loss in the wake of Nehru's death had helped party leaders to stay together. But the loss of the president, more so the vacancy, had come at a stage when the hiatus between prime minister

Mrs Indira Gandhi and the Old Guard, led by the Congress president S. Nijalingappa, was too visible and too wide.

The issue of who would occupy the office of India's president had come to assume importance because Mrs Gandhi believed that the Old Guard was determined to have their own nominee in order to push her out of office. This was convoluted thinking because the president was a Constitutional head who could not dismiss a prime minister so long as he or she enjoyed a majority in the Lok Sabha. On the other hand, it was true that the Old Guard was not happy with Mrs Gandhi and wanted to get rid of her. But they dared not challenge her. As the situation stood at that time, she would have won a vote of confidence in the Lok Sabha hands down.

Still, Mrs Gandhi was worried and determined to have, as India's president, a candidate who would enjoy her confidence. It was not too tall a demand for the prime minister to make. But the dispute at that time was, who would have the upper hand, the prime minister or the party leaders? Mrs Gandhi made the first move. A few days previously at the All India Congress Committee's session in Bangalore (30 July, 1969) she released a note containing some 'stray thoughts'. This was the work of her secretary, P.N. Haksar, known for his leftist views.

The note suggested, among other things, a ceiling on unproductive and conspicuous expenditure, greater economy in public sector undertakings and the prohibition of foreign capital in fields where local knowhow was available. The purpose of the note was to give an ideological twist to the confrontation between Mrs Gandhi and the Old Guard. She wanted to project them in a conservative mould; a bunch of men who did not fit into the progressive and modern India she was trying to build. To her surprise, the Old Guard took no time in accepting the note in toto. Morarji Desai, Mrs Gandhi's specific target, in fact, moved a resolution at the session to accept the note. The backing was unanimous.

Having staved off her challenge on the ideological front, the Old Guard then tried to put Mrs Gandhi in place. They nominated Neelam Sanjeeva Reddy, one of their associates, as the party candidate for the office of president. Their argument was that even during her father's time, the party's Parliamentary Board (where they were in a majority) had the decisive voice in such matters. This was true. Nehru had also been rebuffed, when he had wanted S. Radhakrishnan, then vice-president, to be president of India. The Parliamentary Board had at that time preferred another term for Rajendra Prasad to Radhakrishnan's elevation. The difference was that if Nehru had stood firm, the Parliamentary Board would have given in; nobody ever challenged his leadership. But this was not the case regarding Mrs Gandhi. The Old Guard was openly telling her that they would decide who would be the party's candidate for presidency. For them, her wishes did not count.

Mrs Gandhi was angry over the tactics of the Old Guard and did not hide her disapproval. She said publicly that they would 'pay the price' for having nominated Reddy. (The Old Guard was able to entice Y.B. Chavan on their side to win in the Parliamentary Board). With the help of D.P. Mishra, who was indebted to her for his rehabilitation after her father had driven him out of Madhya Pradesh politics, she struck back at the Old Guard. On Mishra's advice, she stripped Morarji of the finance portfolio, without touching his status as deputy prime minister.

Talking to me at that time, Mrs Gandhi said that the people had returned the Congress to power again and again because they wanted the government to move towards the left and Morarji did not have that approach to economic problems. When I countered that at least he had faith in 'basic values', she snapped: 'Humbug!' In the letter she wrote to him, she said that he had come to be 'identified with certain basic approaches and attitudes' which were contrary to the mood of the nation. Morarji had no choice except to resign from the government.

Before the Old Guard could regain their balance, Mrs Gandhi nationalized fourteen major Indian banks. The cabinet was consulted only perfunctorily and the Planning Commission, which chalked out economic steps, was not extended even that much courtesy. Never had people applauded any economic step as much as they did this one. There was a general feeling that the 'liberal steps' which Mrs Gandhi took would make the country prosperous and improve their lot.

Her stock was high, and All India Radio – which she kept as a government department despite a high-power Commission's recommendation to make it autonomous, on the lines of the BBC – saw to it that she alone stalked the stage. The Congress as a party was nowhere in the picture.

S. Nijalingappa wrote in the diary he maintained: 'There have been demonstrations of taxi drivers, rickshawalas, students, etc. before her house. She addressed them as if she is the only one who works for the poor and she complains against a few individuals. Even the name of Congress is not mentioned.'

Whatever the Old Guard's opinion, the new dress of the left that Indira Gandhi wore, became her well. She went on repeating in almost every speech that she considered it her duty to ameliorate the condition of the common man, and this was more important to her than office. This was populistic politics that no leader before her had tried, but it did carry the promise of a better deal, which for more than 90 per cent of Indians had so far been an empty dream.

It was no sounding of elfin bugles for revolution; she was only making it clear that she stood left of centre while her rivals in the party were far to the right. The CPI read more than personal jealousies in the Congress in-fighting.

When the dominant class is engulfed, says Karl Marx, then we have the synthesis, a new starting point in

development. The CPI thought of making Mrs Gandhi the
jumping board for the implementation of communist
philosophy and put all its weight on her side.

But the party paid heavily because some of its members
went into Mrs Gandhi's fold and became ministers; the
difference between the CPI men and liberal Congressmen
became indistinct as time went by.

18

Notes from Nijalingappa's Diary

CONGRESS PRESIDENT, S. NIJALINGAPPA'S PERSONAL DIARY WAS a scoop which helped me trace events leading to the party's split in 1969.

I never knew he kept a diary. But when I came to know of it, I pleaded with Nijalingappa to loan it to me. At the time of my borrowing the diary, he asked me what I would do with it. I replied that I would make full use of it. I did. The diary was full of his observations on Mrs Gandhi. The burden of his comments was that she was a communist and what she was doing, was to cleave the party 'at the instance of Moscow'. In one diary entry after meeting Ashok Mehta, once a central minister in Mrs Gandhi's Cabinet but later opposed to her, Nijalingappa wrote: 'Ashok Mehta wants the woman to go as he thinks she will sell the country to Russia. This is the feeling among many.'

S.K. Patil of the Old Guard from Maharashtra, went even further, alleging that Mrs Gandhi's secretary, P.N. Haksar, was regularly supplied with a suitcase full of currency notes from the Russian embassy. Haksar was upset by the charge when I asked him for his reaction. 'You know me better,' he said.

But the Old Guard was unable to cope with the propaganda Haksar unleashed, claiming that they belonged to a class that stood in the way of progress. They were painted as having vested interests; as grasping capitalists who were against Mrs Gandhi because she wanted to take steps for the country's betterment. The Old Guard believed that Indira Gandhi had imported the strategy from communist countries to defame their opponents and destroy their credibility. They were convinced that it was all part of the same strategy that communist countries adopted to defame their detractors, the world over.

However, people were happy with the nationalization of banks because of the impression spread that they too would 'get money'. Mrs Gandhi's victory in the Congress was necessary for them. She too needed their backing because she had decided to challenge the Old Guard. After the Congress Parliamentary Board defied her by accepting Neelam Sanjeeva Reddy as the party nominee for the office of president, Mrs Gandhi decided to hit back.

She let it be known that she would support V.V. Giri, who had filed his nomination as an independent candidate with her blessings. He knew of the goings-on within the Congress party and had an inkling that Mrs Gandhi wanted him to stay in the field in case she could not have Jagjivan Ram nominated.

India's intelligence agencies generally complicated matters. This time their information helped Mrs Gandhi to make up her mind. RAW's information was that Morarji and other members of the Old Guard had plans to throw her out. The plan, as spelled out to her, was that after installing Reddy in Rashtrapati Bhavan, fifty Congress MPs would approach the president, express lack of confidence in their leader and suggest that he should ask her to prove her majority in the Lok Sabha. In view of the precarious majority of the Congress party in the House, he would be 'justified' in asking her to do that. Under Article 75 of the Constitution, 'the ministers shall hold office during the pleasure of the president'. Mrs Gandhi's quarters leaked out the intelligence information to make the public believe that the Congress leaders were out to get her.

Reddy was forced to issue a statement: 'The president of India is the Constitutional head, who has no policy and programme of his own. It is the government of the day which chooses the policy and programme to be pursued within the framework of the Constitution.'

Chavan told me subsequently that if Reddy had been elected he would have been as loyal to Indira Gandhi as any other president. Kamaraj too tried to allay fears about pulling her down from the office of prime ministership. He told me that he would not have allowed 'any disturbance' in the prime ministership because the country would have suffered from the fallout.

We will never know whether Reddy, if he had been elected, would have turned her out, or whether the president had the power to do it. The issue about the limits of the president's powers had come to the fore during Nehru's time in a different way: Rajendra Prasad, then president of India, had threatened to act 'on his own judgement' and withhold assent to the Hindu Code Bill, which ensured rights of property and divorce to Hindu married women, hitherto denied.

In the Bill's defence, Nehru wrote to the chief ministers that 'for my part, I am convinced that progress in India must be on all fronts – political, economic and social. Unless this happens, we shall get held up'. At that time, legal experts had opposed Prasad and had said that the president's position was analogous to that of 'a British monarch'. B.R. Ambedkar, who piloted the Constitution as law minister, also described the president as 'occupying the same position as the king under the English Constitution'. Once Prasad knew that his interpretation of the Constitution was wrong, he withdrew the threat. He could not think of harming the country in any way.

V.V. Giri won, but by a small margin (420,077 for, 405, 527 against) and that too only after the counting of the second preference votes, since no candidate had secured two-thirds of the votes polled to ensure a straight win. It was indeed a victory for Mrs Gandhi and for her popular image. However, the majority of Congressmen, despite Mrs Gandhi exerting pressures, had voted for Reddy – 62 per cent in parliament and 75 per cent in the state legislatures. It was the cross-voting of the Congress party, the solid support of the communists and the second preference of those who had voted for C.D. Deshmukh, the third candidate, which ultimately gave Giri the edge over Reddy.

Hurt and humiliated, the Old Guard accepted a unity resolution which was drafted in the prime minister's secretariat but moved by Chavan as his own. Indeed, Chavan's decision to rejoin Mrs Gandhi made all the difference. At one time, he had veered to the side of the party bosses because, as Kamaraj told me, 'Chavan and Morarji came to an understanding that Morarji would be the prime minister till the 1972 polls and Chavan after that.'

Dinesh Singh gave me another version: 'Chavan came to Mrs Gandhi's side because she offered him the prime ministership after 1972 but when she won hands down in the mid-term poll in 1971, she "forgot" the offer. On his part, he dared not ask her to make good her promise.'

Chavan, with whom I later checked these two statements, claimed that Morarji did offer him prime ministership but said, 'Dinesh Singh is telling a lie.' As I found out, Mrs Gandhi never promised anything to Chavan. Kamaraj told me that the reason for Chavan's change of heart was that Morarji wanted to be prime minister even after 1972. 'So, he (Chavan) thought if he had to be number two, then why not to Mrs Gandhi?' He, however, regretted: 'If we had taken action against her before the presidential election, we would have won.'

There is no doubt that Chavan would have tilted the balance. Kamaraj told me: 'If he had come to our side when it came to the crunch, we would have won.'

D.P. Mishra, Mrs Gandhi's strategist, confirmed this. His observation was: 'Once we had won over Chavan, the whole game was over; they would have won if he had gone to them.' Maybe, Chavan had wanted all of them all to stay together and that explained his efforts to keep the party united.

The unity resolution was only a truce. It did not last long. This time the party bosses fired the first salvo by ousting Fakhruddin Ali Ahmed and C. Subramaniam, two staunch supporters of Mrs Gandhi, from the Congress Working Committee. Her supporters convened a meeting of AICC members in Delhi and turned out S. Nijalingappa from the party. The latter's supporters in turn convened a meeting of the Congress party to expel Mrs Gandhi. It was a complete mess now. The eighty-year-old party had begun to totter.

Of all people, it was Vengalil Krishnan Krishna Menon, a former defence minister known for his pro-communist views, who had put Chavan on the conciliation job because of fear that India might disintegrate if the Congress party split.

But no efforts could save the party. Differences between the organizational and parliamentary wings, more so between the personalities on both sides, had become so acrimonious that the party had to split sooner later. But none had thought that it would come so soon, or that 12 November 1969 would be the ominous day.

19

The Taming of the Judiciary

THE SPLIT IN THE CONGRESS PARTY IN 1969 BROUGHT ABOUT A division of sorts in Indian civil society. Some feared it would hurt the country's unity. The division was supposed to be between progress versus reaction. Supporters of Mrs India Gandhi paraded themselves as left of the centre and dubbed the others as 'right-wing'. The word, 'commitment' came into currency at that time to differentiate between those who believed in pro-people policies and those who supported the vested interests. Committed civil servants were those perceived to be loyal to the pro-public sector, socialist pattern of society.

I asked Prime Minister Indira Gandhi one day whether by saying that officials should have a sense of commitment she meant that they should be loyal to a particular ideology, or a party or an individual. She clarified that she had never meant that officials should be doctrinaire in their approach or committed to a party or person. What she had in mind was that public servants should believe in the principles which were enshrined in the Constitution. She cited the example of government servants practising untouchability which was banned under the Constitution. She, however, also added that the persons working in public sector undertakings should have faith in the philosophy of the public sector.

This was only a facile explanation. Her real purpose was to establish personal rule. But the façade of ideology was her forté. Many years later, she had the Preamble of the Constitution amended to include the word 'socialist'. Most civil servants 'changed' their attitude to fit into these new expectations. But the judiciary posed a problem.

The government wanted the judges too to fall in line. Justice A.N. Grover, then a supreme court judge, rang me to inform that the pressure was building up on the judiciary. I was then the resident editor of the *Statesman*. Grover told me that he, along with two of his colleagues, Justice J.M. Shelat and Justice K.S. Hegde, were being superseded because they lacked 'commitment'. Justice A.N. Ray, fourth in seniority, was being appointed the chief justice. He was reportedly in tune with the 'progressive ideology'. The then law minister H.R. Gokhale had even indicated to some that Ray was the next chief justice.

Hegde was next in line to be chief justice. He was considered close to S. Nijalingappa from the Old Guard. Shelat, his senior, had only three months left before his retirement. If Hegde was to be superseded, Shelat would also be vulnerable. Since the proposal was aimed at bringing in the pliable Ray, Grover too had to go. Such was the government's scheme of things.

The evil genius, it was an open secret, was S. Mohan Kumaramangalam, once a Communist Party card holder, who had joined the Congress in the wake of the party's split. Merely a steel minister, he was the main adviser to Mrs Gandhi. But he was a brilliant lawyer. He told me how both he and Gokhale had discussed the matter and had come to the conclusion that they could not let Hegde become the chief justice.

Kumaramangalam said, 'Hegde was a Congress organization man and was always in touch with the Syndicate.

He was not much of a lawyer, but he was a brilliant judge though of a different philosophy. We simply could not have him. And once we had decided to supersede him then why should we have settled for a lesser person like Grover?' Hegde was also the topic of discussion at the Political Affairs Committee meeting of the cabinet. It was noted that he had always taken an anti-government stand and might, if made chief justice, prove to be an impediment in the way of 'progressive' legislation.

Hegde had held the Bank Nationalization Act *ultra vires* of the Indian Constitution on the grounds that the compensation was 'unfairly low'. While the government could legally take over banks, he said, it could not stop their corporate owners from engaging in banking and non-banking business on par with the banks which had been left out of the scheme of nationalization. Little did the Congress realize then that globalization would lead to an unravelling of all those so-called progressive policies one day.

Shelat too was not to the liking of Mrs Gandhi's advisers. He had tilted the balance against the government in the Golakhnath case in which the Supreme Court had held six to five that the fundamental rights enshrined in the Constitution could not be amended, abridged or abrogated by parliament. Since, under Article 19(F), the right 'to acquire, hold and dispose off property' was a fundamental one, parliament had no authority to pass any law which would in any way violate it.

When I drew Kumaramangalam's attention to the allegation that he was pushing Ray's appointment he said that it was wrong to say so. 'The Political Affairs Committee of the cabinet has seasoned persons like Jagjivan Ram and Swaran Singh. They are not taken in easily by anyone.'

Asked if there was any truth in the rumour that at one stage he (Kumaramangalam) was being considered for the office of chief justice, he said: 'None whatsoever. The only thing I was offered in my life was attorney-generalship to which I said no.'

The matter never came up before the cabinet. In the words of one minister: 'We may be consulted about the removal of three clerks from the government but never on subjects like the appointment of the chief justice.'

President Giri, although indebted to Mrs Gandhi for the office, was not happy over the supersession of judges. His suggestion was to appoint J.M. Shelat as chief justice for three months and prepare public opinion to do away with the convention of following seniority for the post of chief justice.

The president told the law minister how, in democratic countries like the USA, Canada and the UK, the question of who the next chief justice should be was not decided by seniority on the Bench. Giri was the government's advocate because Indira Gandhi had made his presidentship possible.

The Constitutional position was clear regarding judges: The president was to consult the chief justice of India 'in the case of appointment of a judge other than the chief justice'. but on the appointment of chief justice the Constitution was silent. Gandhian leader Jayaprakash Narayan wrote to the prime minister:

> The simple fact is that if the appointment of the chief justice of India remains entirely in the hands of the prime minister of India, as has been the case in the present instance, then the highest judicial institution of this country cannot but become a creature of the government of the day.

Mrs Gandhi's reply was:

> The seniority principle has led to an unduly high turnover of chief justices. I take it that no one maintains that the rule of law is safeguarded only by

the principle of seniority. In the appointment of the new chief justice, we have only freed ourselves of a convention which had the sanction neither of the Constitution nor of rationality. It would be atrocious to think that the independence of the judiciary is thereby affected. The outcry and controversy which have attended the appointment seem to me to be wholly misplaced.

At the golden jubilee of the *Matrubhumi* newspaper in Cochin, Mrs Gandhi touched on the controversy again. She said:

A great campaign is being waged, that the executive is out to humble the dignity and authority of the judiciary. We have done no such thing. All that has happened was that we did not bow before the idol of seniority. Seniority is not a law either of nature or of reason. It is certainly not the best guide in any branch of life.

A.N. Ray was appointed the chief justice. Hegde, Shelat and Grover resigned from the supreme court. They warned me in separate interviews: ' You, (meaning the press) are next!' Grover, of the three, was most unhappy. He did not want to resign but had no alternative.

20

A Steel Plant in Visakhapatnam

THE PEOPLE OF ANDHRA PRADESH FELT HURT WHEN THE central government put up steel plants in Bihar, Orissa and West Bengal, but not in their state. They watched the iron ore from Visakhapatnam going out, without any sign of its utilization in their own state. They began to build up pressure when New Delhi was in the midst of installing a fourth steel plant in the country. Visakhapatnam was one of the sites in the list of six. This annoyed the people of Andhra Pradesh all the more. They wanted the plant at any cost. State-wide protests were staged. One person, K. Raguramhia, undertook a fast unto death in Hyderabad.

A person undertaking a fast unto death was, however, nothing new for Andhra Pradesh. It knew how pressure worked. After all, it was only after the death of Potti Sriramulu in 1952 that the States Reorganization Commission was appointed and the government of India pronounced its decision to create a state 'consisting of Telugu-speaking areas of the present Madras state but not including the city of Madras'.

I picked up the trail when the proposal to set up a steel plant in Visakhapatnam in the public sector was finalized and placed before the Union Cabinet. The note for the cabinet, prepared by the Steel Ministry, discussed the pros and cons of different sites but recommended the installation site at Visakhapatnam. This decision was a bit rushed but it was understandable because New Delhi was worried over the deteriorating health of the fasting Raguramhia.

After the cabinet meeting, I went to one of my sources, Fakhruddin Ali Ahmed, to learn about the government's decision. He had disclosed many cabinet decisions to me on previous ocasions.

Ahmed was in his office at his residence. On cabinet meeting days, ministers did not want to meet journalists. The then prime minister Indira Gandhi was very strict and had often lost her temper after reading in the press about what had transpired at a cabinet meeting. She was the one who introduced the practice of ministers returning their cabinet-meeting notepads to the PMO after the meeting.

There was just too much hush-hush surrounding the plant.

Normally, I would have skipped the story. But Raguramhia's fast-unto-death on the one hand and the daily pandemonium in parliament, over the location, on the other, had made the decision on the location of the plant all the more newsy and important.

Fakhruddin's personal assistant recognized me as soon as I entered and sent me in straightaway. Fakhruddin wore his familiar grin on his face. Without beating about the bush, I asked him what happened to the steel plant proposal. He said: 'We accepted it and Visakhapatnam is the location.'

I hastily bade him goodbye and rushed to the office. All that I wanted to know was whether the cabinet had okayed the proposal and which site it had chosen. Once I got my answer I had no reason to linger at Fakhruddin's place. I had already collected the background data and other information earlier, and had kept it ready at my office, in the UNI.

My story, that the Union Cabinet had decided to set up a steel plant in Visakhapatnam, must have landed in newspaper offices around 9 p.m. That was the time when the heads of the news bureau and political correspondents normally called it a day and went home. But some of them had stayed back that night to check if any news agency had anything on the steel plant. My story came in handy to them. They rewrote it and put in their own bylines; not unusual.

My satisfaction was that my story had enabled Raguramhia break his fast. The then Andhra Pradesh chief minister Brahmanand Reddy went to the place where Raguramhia was fasting and showed him the story I had done. He broke his fast. The following day, the newspapers not only carried the decision on the location of the plant but also a picture of a triumphant Reddy giving a glass of juice to Raguramhia.

Members of parliament were furious after reading about the decision in the press. As soon as question hour was over in the Lok Sabha, several of them were up on their feet to attack the government.

The refrain of their criticism was: Why did the government not follow the practice of announcing the decision in parliament when it was in session? I was watching the proceedings from the press gallery, and was confused when I found Mrs Gandhi smile, as if she was enjoying the spectacle.

When the MPs had got their anger off their chests, she got up calmly to say that no decision had been taken. There was a hush in the House. Some press correspondents who had made my story their own looked at me accusingly. I sat impassively because they could not disown the story as the newspapers had printed it under their byline. However, I felt let down. Why did Fakhruddin mislead me? He had never done it before. I went back to his house and waited for him till he came for lunch. I accosted him as soon as he alighted from his car, and asked him why he told me that the proposal to install a steel plant at Visakhapatnam had been accepted when the cabinet had taken no such decision.

Since he was not present at the Lok Sabha when Mrs Gandhi spoke, I filled him in on what had transpired. He repeated that the proposal had been accepted.

Something was wrong somewhere. Mrs Gandhi could not tell a lie to parliament. I went to another minister, Gulzarilal Nanda, to recheck whether what Fakhruddin had reiterated was true. Nanda said the proposal was not accepted, although the installation of a plant at Visakhapatnam was on the Steel Ministry's proposal agenda. When the item was reached, Nanda explained, Mrs Gandhi had suggested deferring it because of too much tension in the air. She said that the government would take the decision after tempers had cooled down. But why had Fakhruddin continued to insist that the proposal had been accepted, I asked Nanda. He said that the normal procedure was to agree to the ministry's proposal. But by the time the item was taken up and the prime minister proposed its postponement, Fakhruddin had left. He wrongly presumed that the proposal had been passed, not knowing that it had been postponed.

Subsequently, I came to know that Mrs Gandhi was happy that the press had got it wrong because it proved that journalists often failed to extract information from her ministers – she did not realize that the newspapers went wrong because one of her ministers had got it wrong!

UNI ran the contradiction. It was embarrassing to do so but there was no alternative.

Some months later, when I went to Hyderabad, many public men, including a few state ministers, complained that the UNI wilted under government pressure and issued a contradiction. The decision, according to them, was taken but changed under pressure from within the Congress party. My credibility remained intact.

I levelled the score with Mrs Gandhi a few years later when I was resident editor of the *Statesman*. She had fixed a two-day cabinet meeting without the presence of officials, saying that she did not want any leakage of important items which the government was scheduled to discuss. After the first day cabinet meeting, I went around and collected every last detail from different ministers. My colleagues also chipped in to help gather all the information about exactly what each minister had said.

Before the start of the second day's cabinet meeting, a frustrated Mrs Gandhi told her colleagues, that it seemed as if Kuldip Nayar himself had been attending yesterday's cabinet meeting!

The Emergency

21

A Nation in Shackles

'PRIME MINISTER INDIRA GANDHI WAS INQUIRING ABOUT your health,' said the Delhi deputy commissioner when he met me in the infamous Tihar jail, outside Delhi, where I had been incarcerated, in late August 1975, during the Emergency.

Mrs Gandhi and I had been friends for years, long before she imposed the Emergency. It was a measure of our closeness and rapport that on one memorable occasion, when she had had her long tresses cut short, she laughingly asked my opinion about whether the new hairstyle suited her. At that time, we were together in the Central Citizens' Committee, which Prime Minister Jawaharlal Nehru had set up under her chairmanship to harness popular support during China's attack on India in 1962. We were in regular contact with each other when I was resident editor of the *Statesman* (1966-74). In the circumstances, and given the background of our meetings, it made no sense that Mrs Gandhi had okayed my arrest. So I was surprised when the police knocked at my door at five in the morning on 25 July. But then I remembered the letter I had written to her three days earlier to point out that the press censorship she had imposed, violated the

Constitutional right of the freedom of expression and was against democratic principles. Years later, her personal secretary, R.K. Dhawan, enlightened me further on the reason for my detention. He told me that the ruling establishment wanted to instil some fear in the minds of the journalists and concluded that they should pick 'the topmost' in the profession. This worked. As the more senior members of the profession were detained, others fell into line, although some 105 of them had assembled in the Press Club, Delhi, on my calling, to criticize the press censorship two days after the Emergency had been imposed.

When the deputy commissioner met me, I had completed one month of detention. He said he had just finished my book, *Distant Neighbours- A Tale of the Subcontinent* and wanted to congratulate me. But he was embarrassed about doing so in jail. We talked for almost two hours about anything and everything except political issues. He turned out to be the son-in-law of a colleague of mine at the Central Government's Press Information Bureau where I had worked for ten years, first as the information officer of Home Minister Gobind Ballabh Pant and then of Lal Bahadur Shastri.

The deputy commissioner wanted to know whether I was comfortable. I told him that the jail was overcrowded and dirty. He said that he could not help that because the number of detainees in the jail was far more than it could accommodate. The lavatory flushes had been systematically destroyed by a group of Akalis who had been in jail earlier in connection with an agitation.

It was late in the evening when the deputy commissioner said goodbye. I told him to thank the prime minister for inquiring after my health. I had lost 10 kilos because I did not like the food. For one thing, there were too many flies, in fact some of them seemed to be practising their swimming strokes on the surface of the watery dal, which was the main dish! I recall, after my release, when I complained to the minister of state for home affairs that the jail was filthy in the extreme, he replied, 'We had not sent you to the five-star Ashoka Hotel.' B.N. Tandon, an officer in the PMO, noted in his diary on the Emergency, that 'nobody dared to take tea with Kuldip Nayar in those days'.

I was present in the Delhi High Court when the two-judge Bench, comprising S.M. Rangarajan and R.N. Aggarwal, read out the judgement to exonerate me from the charges the government had framed against me. The reason I could attend court was that the government had anticipated my release. I was freed two days before the judgement. The government lawyer then argued that, since I had already been released, there was no necessity to deliver the judgement. But Rangarjan said that he had repeatedly inquired from the prosecution if the government was thinking about releasing the detainee, because then he would not take the trouble to write the judgement. Now that he had done so, he would read it out in the court. I was present in the court to say that I wanted to hear the judgement. In his judgement Rangarajan said:

> The facts set out in Mr Nayar's petition had not been challenged. These were that he had never been a member of a political party, had never taken part in a political demonstration, that he had not committed even an ordinary breach of the law, that as a journalist he had an international reputation for his objectivity and that no objection had been taken by the censors to any of his writing after the Emergency. Nothing appeared in the press because of the advice by the chief press censor officer that the judgement would not appear in print....

The main charge framed against me was that I had instigated Muslims at the New Delhi railway station to rise in revolt against the government. How low could the ruling party fall! The real reason for my detention was the weekly column I was writing in the *Indian Express*. The first one I wrote after the Emergency was entitled: 'No, Mr Bhutto, No'. Only Mrs Gandhi's name had to be substituted in place of Bhutto's; otherwise the story of arrests and suppression was the same. The next column was printed on the 4th of July. Praising the American Independence Day, I quoted George Washington and others to re-enunciate the principles of freedom and democracy. In the last one, before I was picked up, I advised undergraduates that, as the future generation of Indian leaders, they should read Voltaire and the Champions of Democracy. Asking students to consider their future vocations carefully, I slipped in a barb advising the younger generation that there was not much of a future in journalism. The government first ruled that none of my writings would appear in the papers. Later, it arrested me to ensure my silence.

There were many foreign dispatches written in my support and to criticize the government. *The Spectator*, London, wrote an edit in my favour:

> The real force of a general problem or crisis strikes us only when the affair comes to have a personal application. Thus it is with the arrest of *The Spectator's* Indian correspondent, Kuldip Nayar, distinguished alike by his career in his own country and his informed contributions to our own columns and those of the *Times*. Kuldip Nayar is merely one of many victims of Mrs Gandhi's state of dictatorship, and he may well have suffered less than many others; but he is our friend and colleague, and we have a special concern for him. In recent months he has, clearly, become more critical of the Indian government than he had been before: the strength of his work for *The Spectator* lay more in his sympathetic exegesis of the difficulties

and problems of Indian government than in any crusading or hectoring quality. Indeed, especially during the Indo–Pakistani war he continually demonstrated rare insight into and understanding of the special difficulties which confronted the Indian government. Before Mrs Gandhi declared her state of emergency, many English papers-including this one, wrote with warm sympathy of the survival of democracy in India which the verdict of the court on Mrs Gandhi's electoral activities seemed, for a brief moment, to demonstrate...

After my release, I tried to pick up the threads from the Press Club meeting I had organized before my arrest. I wanted to organize a protest meeting at the Press Club. Sadly, I could not get even a single pressman to support me.

The Shah Commission, which was appointed to go into the excesses of the Emergency, said that it 'notes with concern the observations made by Shri Kuldip Nayar that there were not many people, even among the senior journalists, to go along with him when he took up the matter of censorship with the Press Council'.

22

The End of the Emergency

IT HAD JUST STARTED TO TURN A BIT NIPPY IN EARLY November 1977. I was coming out of a social function in Delhi when a police officer from my state, Punjab, tapped my shoulder and whispered that the Emergency was being lifted. Unbelievingly, I looked at him. I had met him before but I could not recall his name. My instinct told me that he was telling the truth. But I had also heard that a fresh crackdown was in the offing because the criticism of the government was increasing every day. Prime Minister Mrs Indira Gandhi and her son, Sanjay Gandhi, the extra-Constitutional authority, were the target. Looking at my astonished face the police officer added: 'We have been told to assess what the chances of a Congress candidate in Delhi will be, if elections are held within the next three months.'

He was obviously from the Intelligence Bureau. But he could also have been from the Research and Analysis Wing, RAW. Mrs Indira Gandhi had begun using RAW – meant for espionage activity abroad – to crosscheck all the information she got from the IB.

The Emergency, imposed on 26 June 1975, was eighteen months old. The fear was still there but far less than what it was initially. The press was still gagged but the number of rumours had increased. The nation, which had been in a state of shock, was slowly coming out of its stupor. The worst part was that tyrants had sprouted at all levels – tyrants whose claim to authority was largely based on their proximity to the seat of power. The attitude of the general run of public functionaries was characterized by a paralysis of will to do the right thing. There was no opposition worth the name.

Yet Mrs Gandhi was riding a tiger and it was difficult for her to climb off unless something like elections were to take place so that people could decide what they wanted. How to check, much less confirm, the information given by the police officer was my predicament. This was the type of story where one could not afford to go wrong. I had to be doubly cautious: one, because the government had imprisoned me at the beginning of the Emergency for about four months, and two, the *Indian Express*, where I worked, was in the doldrums, definitely not in any shape to take more government onslaughts. If the story proved wrong, Sanjay Gandhi could even use it as a pretext to close down the paper.

I began the exercise of checking the lead with Kamal Nath. He was a close associate of Sanjay Gandhi and in the know of things. Kamal Nath was a member of the *Express* board which had been reconstituted during the Emergency with K.K. Birla of the *Hindustan Times* in the chair. I had a nodding acquaintance with Kamal Nath since we would run into each other at the *Express* building when he came to attend the Board's meeting. He had once offered me the *Express* editorship on the condition that I toed their line. Even my emphatic refusal had not spoilt our relations.

I knocked at Kamal Nath's residence around 7 a.m. He was still asleep. His wife was sitting in the veranda having tea. She offered me a cup. Hardly had I finished it when Kamal Nath emerged from the bedroom. He was surprised to see me. As he settled in a chair and asked for tea, I put him a straight question: From where was Sanjay Gandhi contesting elections? He was somewhat taken aback. His immediate reaction was: 'Who told you?' Before I could reply, he hurriedly added that 'nothing had been decided yet'.

'Who told you?' The words gave Kamal Nath away. Whatever Sanjay Gandhi's constituency, the one thing that lodged firmly in my mind was that the elections were definitely around the corner. I did not know why Kamal Nath had more or less confirmed the polls. He was probably sure in his mind that someone from his group had already tipped me off and, therefore, it was no use hiding things.

I asked him whether he would be contesting. He said yes, he would be contesting from his old constituency in Madhya Pradesh. What was the hitch, I enquired? He explained that someone had gone to Chandra Shekhar, the young Turk (later India's eighth prime minister), presently detained in Ahmedabad, to persuade him to contest on the Congress ticket. I was amazed at their optimism. How could they even think that a person whom they had kept under detention for more than eighteen months, would join hands with them?

I wanted to know when the elections were being held. Kamal Nath's reply was that it all depended on Chandra Shekhar's reply. Even if he said no they would go ahead because Mrs Gandhi was very keen to have elections in a month or so. My guess, that Mrs Gandhi wanted to dismount the tiger of authoritarian rule, was correct. I changed the subject lest Kamal Nath said something to undermine my growing conviction.

I knew that I should check the story from some other source. But coming from Kamal Nath was like getting it from the horse's mouth. Who else could tell me more? After working for many years in the field you develop an instinct for weighing the authenticity of the information you get. I was sure in my mind that the story of elections was correct. I thought of informing the chief editor because the story had a lot of repercussions but what if he asked me to get confirmation from some other source? I decided to go ahead.

I waited till 11 p.m. before I sent the story to the desk and the different centres from where the *Indian Express* was published. I deliberately delayed the story lest some rival paper should come to know about it and use it as a rumour to finish my scoop. I wrote a straight story to suggest that elections were being held and the Emergency was being lifted within a fortnight. (The Emergency was relaxed not lifted). Political prisoners would be released to enable them to participate in the polls. Naturally, it was the first lead, a thick banner, in all the editions of the *Indian Express*.

It was a little after midnight when Ram Nath Goenka, the owner of the *Express*, rang me up from Bombay. He always saw the first morning edition before going to bed. His query was simple: whether the story was true. He had suffered so much at the hands of the government that he was at the end of his tether – and his resources. If the story was correct, his days of troubles were over. I assured him that the story was correct and the announcement would be made soon. However, elections could be two or three months later, even if the announcement was made now.

After that I went straight to bed. In the early morning there was call from Chief Censor Officer D'penha. We had worked together at the Press Information Bureau (PIB) in Delhi when I was in the government. He told me that the story was mere kite flying. He said, if such a thing had been true, he would have known. Subsequently, he rang me up to convey the government's warning that I could be jailed again. He said that Information Minister V.C. Shukla was furious and had threatened to send me back to prison. I told him that imprisonment was like virginity. After losing it you develop an attitude where it does not matter how many times you are ravished again. I had undergone the rigours of prison and I could bear them again.

Nothing happened to me or to the *Indian Express*. Elections were announced within a few days of my story.

23

A Travesty of Justice

NANI A. PALKHIVALA, AN EMINENT LAWYER FROM MUMBAI, WAS a brilliant man. He was arguing in favour of a bunch of habeas corpus petitions that different detainees had filed in different high courts to articulate their fundamental right of freedom enshrined in Article 21 of the Constitution. They had all been detained under MISA (Maintenance of Internal Security Act), a preventive detention provision, during the Emergency. Earlier, Palkhivala had returned Indira Gandhi's brief relating to an appeal against the Allahabad High Court judgement to unseat her for an electoral offence, and refused to represent her. Palkhivala said India should say goodbye to democracy if the basic freedoms guaranteed in the Constitution were to be snuffed out by the Executive. Fundamental rights were not at the mercy of any government's fiat, he said; they were a product of the people's struggle for independence.

Palkhivala was now appearing before a specially constituted Bench of the supreme court during the Emergency (1975-77). Former attorney-general C.K. Daftary, president of the Bar Association, had, in fact, approached the chief justice of India, A.N. Ray, to set up a Bench of the five senior-most judges to hear habeas corpus petitions. Ray did so, although he was surprised at the request. The four other judges on the Bench were: H.R. Khanna, M.H. Beg, Y.V. Chandrachud and P.N. Bhagwati.

The government raised a preliminary objection: the president had suspended Article 21 when he imposed the Emergency and no action could be brought against it which related to that Article. Daftary argued that the right to freedom did not arise from any particular Article of the Constitution but from the inherent compulsion arising from the principle of the rule of law. The Executive was obliged to honour the principle because the right to freedom – a basic feature of the Constitution – was central to the system. The suspension of the right to enforce Article 21, said Daftary, did not automatically entail the suspension of the rule of law.

Even during the Emergency, 'the rule of law was not and cannot be suspended'. Daftary's case was that Article 21 was the sole repository to the right to life, personal liberty and even the right to move any court. If enforcement of this right was suspended, the detainees had no locus standi.

Justice Khanna was visibly upset over the government's defence that the suspension of fundamental rights was justified during the Emergency. He agreed with Daftary. Bhagwati and Chandrachud too looked distraught and appeared to side with Khanna. However, the scenario changed quickly. Bhagwati was the first to go over to the government's side. Beg was already with Ray. This meant that the case was already going in favour of the government. A few days later, even Chandrachud changed his position, leaving Khanna all by himself. Why did Bhagwati and Chandrachud retract? Was it the fear about the misuse of power the Emergency had created or was it sheer self-interest? Whatever the compulsions of Bhagwati and Chandrachud, the then law minister H.R. Gokhale was happy. All the habeas corpus petitions were rejected 4-1.

In his judgement, Chief Justice A.N. Ray said that when there was public danger, the protective law which gave everyone security had to give way to the interests of the state. Beg said that if the locus standi of detainees was suspended, no one could get the right enforced on their behalf. Chandrachud avoided any comment on the merit of the case. He is still equivocal. He said that president's proclamation of Emergency was final, conclusive and non-justifiable. Bhagwati, an exponent of human rights, was the weakest in his verdict. He said that in the ultimate analysis, protection of personal liberty and supremacy of law must be governed by the Constitution itself and since the persons were detained in accordance with the law, they had no remedy.

Khanna's dissenting judgement was devastating. He said the question was not whether there could be curtailment of personal liberty but whether the law, speaking through the authority of the courts, could be absolutely silenced and rendered mute because of such a threat. It was rumoured that Khanna had written his judgement long before he delivered it, knowing fully well that his verdict would cost him the chief justice's office. If Mrs Gandhi could go to the extent of superceding three supreme court judges because she did not like their judgements and appoint Justice Ray the chief justice of India, Khanna knew that his judgement would seal his fate. But he was ready for punishment. The dictates of conscience as well as law convinced him that the detention during the Emergency was whimsical and motivated.

Khanna's judgement gave hope to the people of India, who had seen even the tallest in the country caving in. After the judgement, Nani Palkhivala wrote in an article in the *New York Times* that Khanna deserved to have a statue erected in his honour because he had dared to speak the truth in the face of all types of danger. Sure enough, the government superceded Khanna and appointed his junior, Beg, as chief justice of India. Khanna did not oblige the government by resigning and by staying on his action emitted a ray of hope in the otherwise dismal performance of the judiciary.

When the Emergency was lifted, Chandrachud was the first one to express his regrets. He could not explain why he had sided with the government. Of what use was his regret? He had not stood up when it counted. Bhagwati was now most critical of the excesses committed during the Emergency but did not say anything about his judgement. He tried to atone for his sins by pronouncing pro-labour and pro-liberty judgements. But no one was willing to forgive him. Both of them remained in the dog-house as long as they were on the Bench. The Supreme Court Bar Association passed a resolution against the two for having delivered the judgement.

Khanna was a hero. Modest and unassuming as he was, he never took the credit for standing alone. His exemplary stance is remembered till today. Of course, so is the stance of Chandrachud and Bhagwati, but for different reasons.

Ray did not stop at the judgement justifying the suspension of fundamental rights. He wanted to utilize the opportunity to rescind the verdict on the basic structure of the Constitution as being inviolable. This came in the way of authoritarian rule. On his own, he set up a Bench of 11 judges to review the theory of the basic structure of the Constitution. Nani Palkhivala probably touched heights that no other lawyer had done, in defending the concept of basic structure. He said it was the soul of the Constitution, which nobody could violate. He asked Ray on whose authority he had constituted the Bench to review the basic structure, which was the Constitutional system itself. Ray replied that some state attorney-generals had requested him to do so. The attorney-general from Tamil Nadu contradicted Ray, saying that no state attorney-general had made such a request. There was no support. He had no choice except to dissolve the Bench.

Chandrachud had a hard time getting appointed as chief justice, because when his turn came, the Janata government had been voted in, having defeated Indira Gandhi. He was saved by Morarji Desai the then prime minister, who was a stickler for form. Morarji did not favour Chandrachud's supercession, knowing well the judgement he had delivered. The then president Neelam Sanjeeva Reddy also played a role because he too felt that tradition and norm were far more important than punishment. He did not want to follow Indira Gandhi's example of destroying the institution; Chandrachud was appointed chief justice.

24

JP's Unrealized Dream

ONE IMAGINED THAT, WHILE IN POLITICAL WILDERNESS, Indira Gandhi must have been haunted by thoughts of what went wrong with her rule; bringing down her two-thirds majority in the Lok Sabha in the 1971 election to a mere 150 in 1977. One also imagined that she would have realized that the methods and the instruments she used to 'meet a serious situation', as she put it, were not only wrong but anti-people.

But the speeches she made during her time in political exile indicated no change in her. She was not repentant and she didn't seek forgiveness from the country. She did not appear to have learnt from her mistakes. Quite the contrary. The worst thing was her continued faith in the methods she had used to commit excesses.

Indira Gandhi's repeated mantra was that she was defeated in 1977 because the people had been 'fooled' by the false propaganda of her opponents. One could not imagine why she wanted to delude herself – if that was what she was doing – because her misrule was an established fact by then. Equally well known were the high-handed and arbitrary actions carried out on her behalf with impunity. Arrests were made based on false allegations, mostly to serve personal and party objectives, or to settle old scores. Yes, it was true that the people had been 'fooled'. The people had been 'fooled' by the lies of her propaganda machine to cover up the rigours of the Emergency. I was unhappy over the defence of Chelapatti Rao, a distinguished editor of the *National Herald*. He wrote a letter in reply to a signed statement in *The London Times* which criticized the paper's appeal for the release of Jayaprakash Narayan. Indira Gandhi's press secretary, Sharda Prasad, had told him to write it.

Indira Gandhi claimed that only 'a few arrests' were made during the Emergency. In actual fact, 100,000 people had been detained according to official records. She would have gone down better if she had said that not even a quarter per cent of India's population (then about 800 million) was put behind bars. And individuals, however respected, hardly mattered to her.

Mrs Gandhi dismissed the commissions of inquiry and characterized their pronouncements as 'all lies'. Subverting the Constitution, forging records, fabricating grounds for detentions, transferring judges, conducting motivated raids in houses, shops and factories, blanketing news, intimidating public functionaries – all these were lies. They must have been a figment of the imagination of some very fertile brains! Or so was Mrs Gandhi's contention.

Take the Maruti Commission report. There was practically no transaction that had been carried out legally: from acquiring land for the project, to the building of bank assets worth crores of rupees, everything had the stamp of the misuse of power and personal aggrandizement. Both Mrs Gandhi and her son Sanjay Gandhi had been found guilty. All were 'lies' according to the two.

Or the Commissions against Bansilal (thrice the chief minister of Haryana), who was now resurrected by Indira Gandhi to save Sanjay. He should not have been ousted from the Congress, she said. To quote only one incident, the Rewasa episode:

Mr Bhanwar Singh's 82-year-old widowed grandmother was burnt alive after being rendered unconscious by police beating. His widowed mother and uncle were subjected to heinous humiliation and torture his other relations were beaten up, their houses burnt or demolished and their crops damaged. Six leading lawyers of Bhiwani who had dared raise their voice against the atrocities were summarily jailed under MISA and a state minister, Mrs Chandravati, was humiliated and sacked for espousing the cause of the victims of Rewasa.

But, according to Mrs Gandhi, these were 'all lies.

She never told the country what the truth was.

Mrs Gandhi had something else in mind. Through the relentless attacks that she been carrying out against the commissions of inquiry, Mrs Gandhi wanted to dilute the impact of the 'guilty' verdict. But she did no mind if, in the process, another institution was devalued – that of inquiry commissions. Those who had begun applauding her – some in the press were crawling even before they had been asked to bend – did not probably realize the harm they were causing to a free society which rested on the credibility such institutions evoked; these were people who did not realize that they were playing with fire. For them the thin line between sycophancy and respect had been erased.

Mrs Gandhi did not spare even the courts. Commenting on a judgement, apparently the one by the Allahabad High Court, she has said it was unjust for a 'petty judge' to ban a former prime minister from contesting elections on flimsy grounds. Many at that time said that the judgement was harsh and that it was like dethroning the prime minister for a parking ticket offence. But she neither added to her stature nor to that of the judiciary by interpreting it as an issue between 'a former prime minister' and 'a petty judge'. Firstly, a judge is a judge, interpreting law and dispensing justice; his status or salary does not lessen his pronouncements in credibility or sweep. Secondly, would Mrs Gandhi, as a former prime minister, have felt better if the judgement had been from a supreme court judge?

Sanjay Gandhi made a mockery of law courts. Every time he appeared before a judge he took along his musclemen, who had become a familiar sight since the Emergency. They ransacked a local court in Dehradun. The judge expressed his exasperation and helplessness. No doubt, it was a reflection on the administration and the UP High Court which did not keep hoodlums away from the court. But it was also an indication of what Sanjay Gandhi and his men believed in. Or, was this his way of saying that the judge trying him was a 'petty' one and should watch out?

Perhaps Mrs Gandhi, who did not utter a word of disapproval, did not realize what would happen to the courts and, for that matter, to other institutions, if all people were to behave like Mr Sanjay Gandhi. It was a game that both sides could play.

True, the people were disappointed with the Janata Party because of its non-performance and infighting. For that reason alone their anger against Mrs Gandhi had lessened. But this did not make those who had no faith in democratic institutions acceptable.

The basic question is, what is permissible in a democratic set-up? Whether Indira Gandhi was repentant or not was between her and her conscience. But what thinking people were worried about was the way she flaunted 'her method' of doing things. She had, in fact, made it plain that India could be ruled through authoritarianism and she could enforce it.

It was a pity that even after watching the futility of authoritarian methods she continued to harp on the 'good' she did during the Emergency. But then that was all she could offer the nation and it was no surprise to see that she had made the Emergency her party's election plank.

~

I recall my last meeting with Jayaprakash Narayan at Jaslok Hospital in Mumbai. A beam of late afternoon sunlight stole in through the half-closed venetian blinds. JP's broad face was etched with lines of fatigue and flecked with dark spots of age. But his eyes were alert with youthful enthusiasm. He spoke softly, as he always did, and talked of convening a meeting, 'not a big one' of intellectuals, administrators and legislators and 'those who wanted to create a new India' – to suggest 'some concrete steps' without making long speeches or entering into intellectual exercises.

I reminded him that he had promised the people *parivartan* (change) and a better lot. 'Unfortunately, my health came in the way,' he said. But he was working on his proposal till the end. A few days later he sent a message to a few people in Delhi, asking them to gather in Patna to discuss the country's problems and how to overcome them.

Even while he fought for his life, JP was conscious of the fact that the work he had initiated remained unfinished. His dream was that the people should participate in administration at all levels and articulate their opinion to the extent that they could influence the government's policies and decisions.

JP had expected the Janata Party, which he had assembled from the different constituents in the opposition, to implement his ideal of total revolution, of making the people the real masters. But before long he realized that the instruments he had selected, those at the helm of affairs, were lacking and did not have faith in his scheme of things.

25

Rising from the Ashes

'SOMETHING MUST BE DONE TO MRS INDIRA GANDHI AND HER son, Sanjay Gandhi.' This was what I heard in the Central Hall of Parliament where members assembled after the 1977 election. Most had been behind bars for nineteen months. Many had suffered the excesses of the Emergency; they were bitter and wanted revenge.

Prime Minister Morarji Desai did not favour any action against Mrs Gandhi. His argument was that the people had punished her by defeating her at the polls. In a democracy, he argued, this was the maximum punishment. Not many agreed with him, not even the top Janata leaders.

The matter came up before both the Parliamentary Committee of the party and the cabinet. At both places, the viewpoint that Morarji had expressed was ruled out. They wanted to try her in a Nuremberg-like trial. The prime minister wrote that no further trial should take place because her defeat was enough punishment. The note was addressed primarily to Home Minister Charan Singh, who had insisted on initiating proceedings against Mrs Gandhi. But Charan Singh had his way and ordered her arrest. It was another matter that the government bungled it up and the magistrate had no option except to let her off. Nothing was produced before the court in support of the order for her arrest; no homework had been done to procure the necessary evidence. It was a shoddy job.

Nonetheless, Morarji Desai was all for setting up a Commission of Inquiry to look into the wrongs done during the Emergency. He personally knew J.C. Shah, a retired chief justice of India, and took no time in appointing him as a one-man Commission. Nobody could question Shah's credentials because he had been a great judge and had refused all the golden handshakes he had been offered after retirement. That the summary of the Commission's proceedings be telecast every night, was the decision of L.K. Advani, then the minister of information and broadcasting. Many said that the daily bashing of Mrs Gandhi on national television evoked sympathy for her. Probably it did, because she returned to power within three years. But the fact remained that the Shah Commission found that 'there was no threat to the well-being of the nation from sources, external or internal', to justify the Emergency. The Commission, in its 3-volume report, said that 'thousands were detained and a series of totally illegal and unwarranted actions followed involving untold human misery and suffering'. Actually Indira and Sanjay had done much worse.

Justice Shah had hardly started looking into the matter when Mrs Gandhi was arrested. He was so angry that he left Delhi by the next flight, returning to Bombay, where he had his chambers. His grievance was that he had not even been informed about her arrest when the entire Inquiry was about the conduct of Mrs Gandhi. Morarji openly apologized to him on behalf of the government. It took a lot of convincing to make Shah resume the Inquiry.

What drove out the Janata government from office was not the Shah indictment but its internal fighting. Morarji and Charan Singh were at loggerheads from day one. The latter felt that he should have been prime minister. Morarji made no bones about his dislike for Charan Singh, whom he called 'Churan Singh', saying he would reduce him to powder. Jayaprakash Narayan, who led the movement against Mrs Gandhi, was given the task of selecting the Janata party leader in parliament. He had nominated Morarji Desai, although Jagjivan Ram had the majority behind him. But then it was he who had initiated the resolution on the Emergency in parliament justifying Mrs Gandhi's action. Charan Singh, according to JP, did not have even a fraction of the party support that Morarji had. Moreover, Charan Singh's lieutenant, Raj Narain, who had won the election petition against Mrs Gandhi in Allahabad, was hobnobbing with Sanjay Gandhi. Morarji knew about this through the IB. In fact, Raj Narain's machinations eventually brought down the Morarji government.

I landed what could have been the biggest scoop of my career when I got whiff of the impending downfall of the Janata government. Devi Lal, elected on a Janata party ticket to become the CM of Haryana, met me at the beginning of the Parliament Session and told me that Charan Singh would go to the extent of pulling down the Janata government to settle scores with Morarji. Devi Lal, whom I knew was a close associate of Charan Singh, said that they had decided to bring the government down and make Charan Singh the prime minister with the help of the Congress. He told me that, on the opening day of the Parliament Session, which was only two days away, one of Charan Singh's associates would resign from the Janata party. This process, of one or more members quitting the party, would continue till the Morarji government was reduced to a minority. Not only that, all of them would support the motion for a vote of no-confidence which the Congress had moved against the Morarji government.

I did not believe Devi Lal and lost one of the biggest stories of my career. Maybe I did not want the Janata government to fall. Mrs Gandhi would be too vindictive if she were to return to power.

What Devi Lal said came true. George Fernandes stoutly defended the Morarji Desai government one day, but roundly condemned it on the subsequent day, because within twenty-four hours, Charan Singh had been offered the prime ministership by the Congress through Sanjay Gandhi.

Raj Narain, who was licking his wounds after Morarji had dropped him from the cabinet, thought he would get his revenge when he made a deal with Sanjay. Little did Raj Narain realize that the Emergency crowd would come back to power.

The Congress was at wits' end. It had wanted the government to fall but it did not realize that it would happen so soon and so suddenly. The party had not yet prepared for elections. Y.B. Chavan, who had moved the motion for a vote of no-confidence, was nonplussed. I asked him why he looked distressed. In reply, he said: 'Kuldip, we had gone out to hunt a fox and have killed a tiger. What can we do?'

Morarji resigned from the prime ministership but not from the leadership of the Janata parliamentary party. President Neelam Sanjeeva Reddy did not give Jagjivan Ram, the deputy prime minister, a chance to form the government. He said that the Janata had been once defeated in the House and he could not, therefore, ask Jagjivan Ram to try to form the government on behalf of the Janata. Technically, Reddy was correct. But the real reason for his refusal was not legal or moral but a manifestation of the old rancour which he had nurtured from the time when the Congress had selected him as the official candidate to contest the office of president in the wake of Zakir Hussain's death, and Mrs Gandhi's group, including Jagjivan Ram, had supported the independent candidate, V.V. Giri.

As expected, the Congress withdrew support from Charan Singh. But he became the officiating prime minister. Before appointing him, Reddy sounded Sheikh Mohammad

Abdullah, the chief minister of Kashmir, to head the caretaker government. The Constitution gave the president complete power to nominate anyone till an elected government was in position. After the Sheikh's refusal, Reddy's choice fell on Charan Singh. While appointing him, Reddy also set a precedent that the outgoing prime minister, without even enjoying the support of the majority, would remain in power till fresh elections were held. That was the end of those who were once united in their fight in ousting Mrs Gandhi.

Once I asked J.P. whether Mrs Gandhi would ever stage a comeback. He did not reject the idea but added: 'She will never be a dictator again. For that matter nobody will, he said emphatically.

Mrs Gandhi returned to power in 1980. She brought back all the men who were part of the Emergency apparatus. She rejected the Shah Commission's recommendations and put the 3-part report on the Home Ministry's shelf. The National Police Commission report was also put in a box because the Commission had been appointed by the Janata government. Whatever work the Janata party had done was undone. The government saw to it. Many officials got promoted in the process. But the Emergency-type of tyranny was gone. She had learnt some lessons at least.

Tremors in the
Subcontinent

27

The Father of Pakistan's Atomic Bomb

MUSHAHID HUSSAIN, EDITOR OF *MUSLIM,* WAS AT THE AIRPORT to receive me. This was on 27 January, 1987. Although we had been friends for years, I was still a bit surprised to see him. But then I assumed that he had been touched by my travelling all the way to Islamabad to attend his wedding. The moment he embraced me, he whispered in my ear: 'I have a *khas* (special) present for you.' I told him not to have bothered, that it was my privilege, not his, because it was he who was getting married, but I wondered what he meant.

The suspense however, was over soon.

'Dr A.Q. Khan will meet you today,' Mushahid said. No doubt, this was the best gift he could have given me because I had been vainly pursuing Dr Abdul Qadeer Khan, the father of the Pakistan bomb, for many years. Mushahid had arranged for me to lunch with Fakhar Imam, then a minister in General Zia-ul-Haq's Cabinet. Fakhar and his wife, Chandi, were close friends of mine. They were happy to see me but had no idea about my mission. Mushahid rang me at their place to inform me that the interview had been fixed for 6 p.m. and that he would pick me up from my hotel.

Khan lived in a bungalow in a locality just outside Islamabad. It was starting to get dark and the hills silhouetted against the sky were becoming more visible. Mushahid switched on the headlights of the car. Anyone from Khan's bungalow, which was built atop a small hillock could see the vehicle driving up. The area was littered with security-men and they, I believed, had beaten up a French journalist a few days earlier for daring to travel on the same road we were using. Khan's house had an ordinary entrance, no high gate, no grill, no automatic devices. A few men in plainclothes, and a couple in khaki, stood guard. None stopped me. None even asked my name, much less frisked me. They greeted Mushahid and talked to him. It was odd. The country's most sought-after scientist was receiving an Indian visitor who was not even made to pass through a detection device! It was obvious that they had been told about me and my meeting.

Khan was standing in the veranda to welcome us. He greeted me thus: 'I am your fan. And I read you regularly in the Pakistan press.' I thanked him for his interest. He led us to the sitting room, behind the veranda. A small round table with three chairs had been placed in the room. Large windows opened out onto a lovely garden making for idyllic scenery. We had barely settled down in our chairs when a lady, a foreigner, wheeled in a trolley laden with food. I knew Khan had married a Dutch woman when he was in Holland working in a nuclear plant.

After we were introduced I joked with her, wondering how she had intuited my fondness for upside-down pineapple pudding. I told her I had not eaten it since leaving Northwestern University in Evanston, near Chicago, from where I earned an M.Sc in Journalism. Khan also introduced me to his two daughters, who were both in skirts. After all three of them withdrew, Khan personally poured the tea and I looked at him closely. He seemed like a person who was pleased with himself. He had been working on the nuclear bomb ever since Prime Minister Indira Gandhi had authorized a nuclear test in India in 1974. Her counterpart, Zulfikar Ali Bhutto, had said soon afterwards that Pakistan would even eat grass to get the bomb. Khan was the cynosure of all eyes in Pakistan, a person who would give the country parity with India.

At the age of 51, his face was more weathered than I had expected. The heavy-framed spectacles he wore gave his appearance a touch of priggishness. He had come a long way from his days in Bhopal where the Partition of India had bruised his sensitivity to such an extent that he had vowed to wreak vengeance on the Hindus for having rendered the Muslim community weak and helpless.

When I told him that he was the most important person in Pakistan, he was overwhelmed. I told him that my purpose in interviewing him was to project the real Khan – his achievements, his struggles, his family life. In reply to my query about his scientific pursuits, he brought me a copy of the *Hurriyat*, an Urdu magazine published by the *Dawn* group of newspapers from Karachi. The *Hurriyat* issue, he said, contained more or less everything about him. As I hurriedly glanced through the magazine I found a picture of his wife and daughters. Mushahid had indicated to me beforehand that I could not take down notes, nor could I use a tape-recorder. I had to reproduce my story from memory. This was tough because I would not be able to corroborate what Khan had said unwittingly.

What struck me about him during our short conversation was that he used too much 'I'. His face would glow with happiness whenever I praised him or talked about his achievements. I had heard he was an egoist and he matched the description every inch. I lauded his qualifications, acknowledging that he was the only scientist in the subcontinent with a doctorate both in physics and metallurgy. He felt gratified. But I annoyed him when I made a passing reference to the time that he had been hauled up by the Dutch courts for having 'stolen' information from one of the nuclear laboratories. He raised his voice to deny the charge, adding that the court had cleared him.

The question of whether India had tried to barge into the secret Pakistan nuclear plant pleased him. Laughing, he said that New Delhi had sent some spies, one of whom was a major in the Indian Army. But they were all arrested. My entire interview technique was directed towards establishing beyond doubt whether Pakistan had made the bomb. He skirted all such questions. He would brush me off whenever I tried to be specific. It seemed to me that he had been allowed to give me an interview. But, at the same time, he had been cautioned not to say anything specific.

I thought I would provoke him; egoist that he was, he might fall for the bait. He did. I concocted a story, saying that when I was coming to Pakistan, I had run into Dr H. Sethna, the father of India's bomb, who had asked me why I was wasting my time because Pakistan had neither the men nor the material to make the bomb. Khan hit the roof and began pounding the table: 'Tell them we have it, we have it.'

Mushahid was taken aback at this disclosure and looked distraught. I followed up Dr Khan's announcement with the remark that it was easy to claim but it had to be corroborated. There was no test conducted so far to confirm that Pakistan had the bomb.

Khan said: 'We have already tested the bomb in our laboratory. Haven't you heard of a prototype plane flying with the help of a simulator? We do not have to explode the bomb to know its potency. Sensitive and advanced instruments in a laboratory can show the scale of explosion. We are satisfied with the results.'

Thus Khan said what he should have withheld. This is what I felt and certainly what was written all over Mushahid's face. Probably, Khan had been told to give a hint but not to confirm specifically that Pakistan had the bomb. He had gone beyond what he was instructed to say. My task was over. I had wanted to know whether Pakistan had made the bomb; Khan had confirmed it.

India had carried out its Operation Brass Tacks exercises right on the Pakistani border in January 1987 and Islamabad wanted to send a warning to New Delhi). In a fit of anger Khan went beyond his brief. In any case, once the information was out Khan and I were relaxed. Mushahid looked worried.

Khan now talked like a member of the ruling elite. He warned me: 'If you ever drive us to the wall, as you did in East Pakistan, we will use the bomb.' What he was trying to convey was that if Pakistan suffered any military reverses in a conventional war against India, it would not hesitate to use the bomb. President Musharraf confirmed this some fifteen years later.

I wanted to know the technical aspects of the bomb; some scientific data. Khan said he had written two articles which explained the type of bomb Pakistan produced. He gave me a copy of both articles. It was easy to put meat to the story. The meeting had lasted only half an hour but had disclosed all.

The first remark Mushahid made to me in the car was: 'He has spilled the beans. What story will you do? Tell me.'

Mushahid was worried. He said he had to live in the country, and the story should not get him into trouble. I offered not to write the story if it would put him in any danger. He kept quiet and did not speak the rest of the way. He was lost in his thoughts. In any case we were meeting for dinner. He dropped me off at my hotel where I immediately reached for a piece of paper to jot down Khan's words. My memory stood me in good stead. At the dinner, Mushahid looked worried. Khan was not supposed to spell out things as he had. For a long time Mushahid never told me that this meeting had been pre-arranged, but I suspected so all along.

Many years later, when I told Mushahid I was writing a book and wanted more details of the interview with A.Q. Khan, he said he was doing one himself.

I asked him whether the interview I had with A.Q. Khan had been set up, to give India a message. He said, yes, it had.

28

Explosions in the Media

I MET S.K. SINGH, THEN INDIA'S HIGH COMMISSIONER TO Pakistan, the day after I interviewed Dr A.Q. Khan. I did not tell him anything about the interview because I wanted Khan's sensational disclosure, claiming to have made the bomb, to be my scoop. The only paper to which I offered to sell the story was *Dawn*. When I met Hamid Haroon, a top executive of *Dawn* in Karachi, I asked him if they would like to run the interview. 'Keep us out,' he said. 'It is too hot.'

One day before my return to India, I was in Lahore when Shyam Bhatia of *The Observer*, a weekly paper appearing from London, rang to enquire about my stay in Pakistan. He knew about my visit but not that I had met Khan. When I told him that I had interviewed Khan, his first reaction was that of disbelief and then he wanted to know the full story. I knew my phone was tapped. I asked him if his paper would be interested in Khan's interview. He said that it all depended on what I had got. He promised to check. On my return to Delhi, he conveyed his paper's interest in the story to me.

I found *The Observer* a stickler for details. Even when I faxed the story, it wanted me to send them my notes. I had already told them that I was not allowed to take down notes,

nor to record Khan. I posted them the papers on which I had
jotted down the details of what Khan had said. It was all from
memory. Subsequently, there were many other telephone
conversations between me and *The Observer* office on the story.
The paper was justifiably cautious because Mushahid Hussain
had already said, under pressure from his government, that
no interview had taken place and that I had merely
accompanied him there to deliver an invitation for Mushahid's
forthcoming wedding. *The Observer* wanted to be doubly sure
because of a report that an American newspaper had been
offered the same story, but had turned it down because they
doubted the veracity of the interview. I did not know who
offered them the story. I certainly had not.

The reason why I was keen for the write-up to appear
abroad was because in our part of the world people considered
a disclosure more authentic if it first appeared in foreign
countries, particularly in the UK. It took me one month to
convince *The Observer* to run the interview. The day *The
Observer* ran the story was the day when our national budget
appeared in the press. My anticipation of poor timing was
correct. My clients – the 70-odd papers which bought my
service – did not run the bomb story as the first lead. Still it
attracted attention. The publication in *The Observer* gave the
story the authenticity – and controversy – it deserved.
Mushahid's retraction did hurt me a bit but I could appreciate
his compulsions in Pakistan. Fortunately, he printed the story
in his own paper and wrote an edit on the interview to argue
that Pakistan should tell the entire world that it had the bomb.
It would send a message to New Delhi, he argued. At that
time, India was conducting, to Pakistan's dismay, a military
exercise codenamed Brass Tacks very near the border.

Not knowing the background, the Pakistanis were angry
and demanded Mushahid's head for helping the 'enemy' and
for telling a Hindu about the bomb. Many asked that
Mushahid be tried for the 'treason' he had committed. I could

not understand why there was such a furore. I was confident that General Zia-ul-Haq would have been consulted at some stage. As I learnt subsequently, he had actually okayed the interview in advance. But he had also made it clear that the fact of Pakistan possessing the bomb should not be disclosed under any circumstances.

Khan had gone beyond the brief. It was clear to me from Mushahid's response in the car that Khan had spilled the beans. Khan did not mean to react but when I said that Pakistan had neither the men nor the material to make the bomb, he was provoked into revealing more than he should have. Zia tried to retrieve the situation when he told *Time* magazine that Pakistan was only a screwdriver away from the bomb. This did not undermine the disclosure because by then the cat was out of the bag. Pakistan's predicament was that the bomb story was published during the same week that its Aid Bill was put before the US Congress for approval. I had no knowledge of the Bill. The timing of my story was pure coincidence. In the meanwhile, Senator John Glenn rang me from Washington to confirm what Khan had said. Still, in the midst of doubts, President George Bush senior cleared the way for aid to Pakistan by certifying that Pakistan did not have the bomb. I think that politics played a role because the US president had with him the reports of his intelligence agencies which declared unequivocally that Pakistan had made the bomb.

If *The Observer* had been less particular about authenticating the story it would have been published much earlier. At least, the charge of conspiracy with New Delhi had not been hurled at me. Someone asked Prime Minister Rajiv Gandhi whether India had conspired with Kuldip Nayar to do the bomb story on the eve of the US Aid Bill. Rajiv replied : 'We can conspire with anyone but not Kuldip Nayar.'

Khan then went to the British Press Council to allege that there was no story and that Nayar had used a social call to circulate a canard through *The Observer*. The paper fought the case and both of us, the paper and I, were exonerated. In its observation, the Council said that it had no reason to disbelieve my version. Khan's petition was rejected.

Islamabad did not give up. It had a book published in which it was alleged that Pamela Bordes, an Indian model, was used by Kuldip Nayar to seduce *The Observer* editor as a way of ensuring the publication of the bomb story. The Press Trust of India picked up the Pamela portion from the book and ran it a couple of years later. I threatened to sue the agency. The agency withdrew the story but never expressed regret. This was a new kind of journalism: to disseminate defamatory material and to refuse to express any regrets. I left it at that because the agency had withdrawn the story after all. The Pakistan High Commission in Delhi also sought to punish me by refusing to issue me a visa for nearly five years.

Some Pakistanis believe to this day that I wronged their country by disclosing their possession of the bomb. But, maybe, I helped them because they ended up getting the best of both worlds: they got the aid from the US *and* they had the bomb in their basement!

29

The Superpowers Join the Fray

I SOUGHT THE HELP OF LIEUTENANT GENERAL HARBAKSH Singh, the hero of the 1965 war against Pakistan, to analyse the daily briefing by the Defence Ministry on the pace of the Bangladesh operation. He was once head of the East India Command in Calcutta and knew the East Pakistan terrain intimately. So knowledgeable was he about what was happening in East Pakistan, that he could provide all the background to the daily briefing on the progress of the war. Everyday I would write a war dispatch after being elucidated by him and byline it, 'by a military expert'. The dispatch aroused attention in high quarters. One day, Ashok Mehta, a former minister in Indira Gandhi's Cabinet, even phoned me to find out who the expert was.

Indian troops moved in fast towards Dhaka and soon established contact with the liberation forces inside East Pakistan. But it was not until 6 December, 1971 – the day India recognized Bangladesh – that a joint command of the Mukti Bahini and the Indian Military came into being. Once Feni, an important rail-cum-road communication point, fell, Indian forces were able to accelerate their advance. A beleaguered Jessore – the BBC referred to it as 'Pakistan's Stalingrad' – surrendered on 7 December.

For the first time during the war, India used helicopters on a large scale and ferried troops across rivers which were still under Pakistan's control. The Sylhet Garrison was isolated and the river Meghna was crossed on 11 December. The same day, a paramilitary battalion was dropped near Tangail; thus foiling Pakistan's attempt to destroy bridges and delay the Indian advance.

The rest of the war belonged almost entirely to the Engineers Corps. They were the ones who had to build bridges and provide other facilities to take tanks and heavy guns across the rivers and rivulets that criss-crossed the area. Although India began tightening the noose around Dhaka, it was still taking longer than expected. Not many Pakistani troops were withdrawing and they looked like they were fighting a last-ditch battle outside Dhaka. Moscow expressed concern over the 'slow pace' of the Indian forces. It did not want Bangladesh to become another Vietnam. Post-haste to Delhi came Soviet official, Vasily Kuznetsov, first deputy minister of foreign affair, to force India to finish the operation quickly. He was, however, relieved to find that the Pakistani forces were retreating and that the hostile Bangladesh population was pushing them. He could see that it was only a matter of three or four days more.

Meanwhile, Pakistan frantically contacted America for the supply of arms and ammunition. Washington accepted the request and thought of ways to deliver them in the face of India's blockade of Pakistani ports. Asked by correspondents whether the US would respond, President Richard Nixon's press secretary simply said: 'There is no news.' This reply was in contrast to an earlier statement by Washington claiming that it would stay neutral in any armed conflict between India and Pakistan. New Delhi noted this change with worry.

India heard from its mission in Washington that Nixon was considering invoking the 1964 Mutual Security Pact between America and Pakistan to give Islamabad military assistance. Mrs Gandhi took the first opportunity (12 December) to warn the US at a public meeting:

> I hear that some countries are trying to threaten us and reminding us that they also had treaties and agreements with Pakistan. I did not know this earlier because whatever agreement there was, as far as I know, had been forged to form a pact against communism. It was not a pact to fight democracy. It was not against the voice of justice. It was not meant to crush the poor. But if it was so, then they told a big lie to the world.

Nixon first sent a 'warning' to India and then ordered the Seventh Fleet, led by the nuclear-powered aircraft carrier, *Enterprise*, to go to the Bay of Bengal. Information about this came first from Moscow, which had monitored a message to the Seventh Fleet in the Tonkin Gulf off the coast of north Vietnam. The Indian Embassy in Washington had warned New Delhi about it. A senior US marine officer had unwittingly revealed it in a conversation with an Indian Embassy official a few days earlier. An Arab diplomat in New Delhi also told our foreign office about the Seventh Fleet moving to the Indian Ocean.

Pakistan was unhappy with the US because it was not giving 'any concrete assistance'. Islamabad argued with Washington that action under its security treaty with Pakistan was not limited to the 'aggression' by communist countries but extended to India. Washington did not spell out why the Seventh Fleet was being moved to the Indian Ocean. First, it was explained that it was coming to evacuate 300 Americans from East Pakistan and then it was rumoured that it wanted to rescue the Pakistani forces. The second explanation sounded credible because General A.K. Niazi, commander of the Pakistan forces in East Pakistan, talked to Indian commanders about the right to evacuate his men.

According to the famous American columnist Jack Anderson, who based his views on unpublished US documents in his possession, the American purpose was four-fold: (a) to compel India to divert both ships and planes to shadow the US Task Force; (b) to weaken India's blockade of East Pakistan; (c) to divert the Indian aircraft carrier *Vikrant* from its military mission, (d) to force India to keep planes on advance alert to thwart action against Pakistani ground troops. The evacuation of American citizens was clearly a secondary mission' Mr Anderson stated and wrote that the evacuation was more a 'justification than a reason' for the movement of the Seventh Fleet.

Pakistan was also banking on China's intervention. But the latter only doled out threats. A few troops were exhibited along the India–China border in the North-west, without taking any hostile position. Islamabad conveyed to Beijing that it felt let down. Yet nothing moved it. Pakistani forces were sure of China's intervention. In fact, when India dropped paratroopers in one area near Dhaka, many Pakistani soldiers stepped out of their bunkers to cheer them, taking them to be Chinese who had come to their rescue. Once they realized that no foreign assistance was forthcoming the Pakistani soldiers lost heart.

When the surrender took place, New Delhi heaved a sigh of relief because the then foreign minister Swaran Singh had phoned from New York saying that it would be difficult to stall a UN resolution which might brand India as aggressor and suggest sanctions against it. The Soviet delegation, on the other hand, went on pressing him to ask New Delhi to hurry up with the Bangladesh operation. Niazi went to the US Consulate in Dhaka three days before the surrender to find out whether America would intervene. When told that America had no intention of doing so, Pakistan first offered

India a ceasefire and then unconditional surrender (15 December) to the joint command of Indian forces and the Mukti Bahini. Niazi wanted to deal only with the Indian Army but New Delhi insisted that the operation was conducted by India and Bangladesh jointly and hence the surrender had to be to the joint command.

India purposely sent Lieutenant General Jacob, a Jew, to negotiate the surrender terms. However, the formal surrender was before Lieutenant General Jagjit Singh Aurora, GOC-in-C of the Indian and Bangladesh forces in the Eastern sector. The Pakistani prisoners in the East totalled 91, 498 – with 56,998 regulars, 18, 287 paramilitary and 16,213 civilians.

The Arab countries being Muslim countries, had sided with Pakistan, and propagated the news that India had made Muslim forces surrender to a Jew. True, India helped Sheikh Mujib-ur-Rehman and his supporters free themselves from Pakistan but too much should not be made of this because it was only a matter of time before Bangladesh would have been free. The alienation of Bengalis was to the last man. It might have been a long struggle, but the independence of Bangladesh was a foregone conclusion. If India had not helped him, Mujib would have procured arms and assistance from other sources because he was determined to free his country from Islamabad's bondage.

30

The War with Bangladesh

I FIRST LEARNT OF INDIA'S INVOLVEMENT IN THE BANGLADESH liberation struggle in early 1971. A BSF officer I met in Jalandhar claimed that he had himself participated in the raids carried on inside what was then East Pakistan. He said there were others from the Border Security Force engaged in the 'same operation'. The modus operandi was simple: some of the BSF men from the forces station in the North-East had joined the Mukti Bahini. This was a band of Bangladeshis fighting the Pakistan Armed Forces to free Pakistan's Eastern wing and convert it into an independent country.

Unbelievingly, I checked the information with my sources and found that the officer's contention was correct. Indeed, India was helping the Mukti Bahini with men and material throughout its insurgency, nearly ten months before Bangladesh became free. However, there was no mention of it anywhere, much less in the press. What was printed was that refugees from East Pakistan were pouring into West Bengal to escape the 'atrocities' committed on them by the Pakistani forces. This was also true. The number of refugees who had collected in West Bengal was 20 lakhs. Along with stories of refugees, there would be, once in a while, an account of the brave fight put up by the Mukti Bahini against the Pakistani forces, always described as 'ruthless'. Stories about the Mukti Bahini were datelined Mujibnagar. I must admit that it took me sometime to discover that Mujibnagar was part of Calcutta. Even then, I never allowed the *Statesman* in Delhi – where I was editor – to say where Mujibnagar was. For our readers it was a small town at the centre of operations in East Pakistan, from where the indigenous uprising was being guided.

One day, *The New York Times* correspondent, stationed in New Delhi, dropped in at my office and asked me straight-out whether I knew that Mujibnagar was only a part of Calcutta. Before I could respond, he asked me why the Indian press did not disclose its location and whether there were some official instructions not to write about it. I told him that there were no such government restrictions, nor did the Indian press function that way. The government would not dare tell the press what to publish or not to because the freedom of the press was a foregone conclusion.

However, I admitted that everyone voluntarily fell in line when it came to what was considered 'national interest'. The uprising in East Pakistan against Islamabad was one example of India's interest because Pakistan was considered an adversary. The only reason I could give off-hand for doing this was that we were 'too near the slavery' or 'too near independence'.

It might seem like an exaggerated notion now but it counted with the press and, for that matter, with all segments of Indian society.

It is difficult to say at what stage India decided to go the whole hog with Sheikh Mujib-ur-Rehman, who was heading the freedom struggle against Pakistan. But it was clear that the unending flow of refugees from East Pakistan was one of the factors that made New Delhi intervene. Still, it was important to get international opinion on India's side. Prime minister Indira Gandhi selected Jayaprakash Narayan, the Gandhian leader, as her representative and sent him to America, the UK and other countries to highlight the humanitarian angle – the tragic plight of the refugees who had been forcibly turned out from their homes. The then foreign minister, Swaran Singh, hinted to forums abroad about creating a 50-mile belt along the East Pakistan border for the temporary settlement of the refugees under the aegis of the UN, until a permanent solution was found. Both America and Britain rejected the proposal.

The refugee factor was real but Indira's assistance to freedom fighters in Bangladesh was not that altruistic. I would pick up evidence of this off and on.

Mrs Gandhi personally went to Moscow to seek its help. But the Soviet Union did not want to get involved, although it was India's closest friend. Before Mrs Gandhi's arrival in Moscow, the then president Leonid Brezhnev left the capital. Soviet prime minister Andrei Gromyko met her and apologized on behalf of Brezhnev who, he said, had gone on vacation. She told him to convey to his president that she would stay on till he returned to Moscow. Brezhnev returned the following day. My assessment was that she had decided to intervene in the Bangladesh uprising before she visited Moscow. The purpose of her meeting Brezhnev was to get the Soviet Union's assurance of coming to India's assistance if China intervened in the Bangladesh War. Beijing had already said in a public statement that it would help Islamabad in East Pakistan.

The Indo-Soviet Peace Treaty signed subsequently between New Delhi and Moscow said that any attack on India would be considered an attack on the Soviet Union.

When the editors of the national dailies were invited by the secretaries to the Government of India for a meeting it was more or less confirmed that Indira's personal intervention was not far away. Sometime in October 1971, the government convened a meeting of local editors at the residence of the then foreign secretary T.N. Kaul. They were half-a-dozen other secretaries. They first thanked us for not disclosing where Mujibnagar was situated and for going along with what the Government of India was doing. One editor asked if it was too late to help establish the Commonwealth of Pakistan, where both wings could enjoy an autonomous status within Pakistan. His argument was that East Pakistan was 'a bottomless pit' and would turn against India if she did not give it large economic assistance regularly. 'We do not have that much money,' he said. Secretary K.B. Lall said in reply that some of them would agree with this point of view but it was too late. Mrs Gandhi had already taken the decision. The die had been cast, and war was only a matter of time.

One piece of advice by Moscow to New Delhi before the beginning of the war, was to finish the operation quickly. It did not want hostilities to be prolonged lest there were complications. It was Moscow's belief that America would jump into the fray if the war was prolonged. Indira Gandhi conveyed this assessment to General Sam Manekshaw who was appointed the top commander for the Bangladesh War.

India's plan was to outflank Pakistan's prepared positions along the border by moving rapidly to the Meghna and Padma rivers and reaching Dhaka. However, after the Bangladesh War, a retired military commander in Delhi alleged that the conduct of the operation in the early days did not suggest that Dhaka was the main target and that too much time was wasted in capturing worthless targets of no military value in the north.

Islamabad was led to believe that New Delhi had planned only a limited action. General A.K. Niazi, the army commander of East Pakistan, admitted during interrogation after the surrender that he had not expected a major Indian attack and had imagined that Indian efforts would be only to capture a chunk of territory for the establishment of a

Bangladesh government. This was the reason, he explained, for his initial deployment of troops and his decision to keep the battle close to the border. But when Indian forces bypassed the fortified Jessore city and when they looked like they were racing towards Dhaka, Niazi realized that if ever there was a plan to 'free' some territory, it had been discarded.

But by then, it was too late for him to change his strategy.

31

The Birth of Bangladesh

THE NINETEEN SEVENTIES' PAPERS, RELEASED BY THE US FROM its archives, reveal that, following its liberation from Pakistan, Bangladesh wanted to establish a confederation between the two countries. This disclosure was based on the information that the American Consulate in Dhaka had sent to the state department in their dispatches. The Consulate based its thesis on the talks Pakistan president Zulfikar Ali Bhutto had with Sheikh Mujib-ur-Rehman, the founder of Bangladesh, when the latter was still Pakistan's prisoner.

The American Consulate was wrong. It postulated such a possibility based on the prevailing rumours of the day. The facts were different. After taking over the reins of Pakistan from General Yahya Khan, who was responsible for Pakistan's debacle in what was then East Pakistan, the first thing Bhutto did was to talk to the Sheikh.

Mujib-ur-Rehman was flown in a helicopter to a dak-bungalow near Rawalpindi where Bhutto occupied the presidential house. Bhutto wanted some links between Pakistan and Bangladesh. But the Sheikh said he could not commit to anything until he visited Bangladesh and talked to his colleagues.

The Bangladesh War had ruptured diplomatic ties between New Delhi and Islamabad. One had to go through the Swiss Embassy for entry into Pakistan. I sent in my request to Bhutto whom I had met many a time earlier. My visa was granted immediately.

I met Bhutto first. This was the conversation which I recorded on tape. Bhutto said:

On 23 December when we (he and Sheikh Mujib-ur-Rehman) met for the first time, Mujib took out the Koran and said, 'I am a good Muslim. I still want Defence, Foreign Affairs and Currency to be central subjects between the two regions.' On 27 December, when we met for the second time, he was very vague. He said: 'I cannot tell you the number of subjects to be given to the centre and what kind of subjects, but I want to retain some links.' I (Bhutto) was sceptical. I told Mujib: 'As you know, you are saying this here and I take you at your word, but when you go there, see the atmosphere and see all the young men with rifles around you and having come back from the grave, you won't be able to do it. But even if you maintain some fictional links, I would be satisfied.' He (the Sheikh) was positive. 'No, No,' he said, 'I am the leader – *main leader hoon, main theek kar donga*' (I am a leader, I shall set things right) and that sort of thing. You know, I like him. The point is that there are so many problems and I don't think he bargained for half of these.'

The Sheikh, whom I recorded after Bhutto, had a different version:

I had learnt from my jailer, a God-fearing man, that Bangladesh had been liberated. Therefore, when I was removed from jail, I suspected that it must be for the purpose of holding talks. I thought I would not indicate any prior knowledge of the liberation of Bangladesh. Within a couple of days of my arrival at the dak bungalow, Bhutto appeared there one afternoon. I asked him: 'Bhutto, how are you here?' He said: 'I am the president of Pakistan.' I began laughing and said: 'You, Bhutto, Pakistan's president? That place belongs to me; you know I won the majority of seats in the Pakistan National Assembly.' As if he wanted to frighten me, he said that he was also the chief martial law administrator, and added: 'I have come to talk to you.' To this, my reply was that I would not talk unless he were to say that I was free. He said 'yes' and so we talked. He blamed Yahya for all that had happened, although I knew that he (Bhutto) had been at the back of everything. He really wanted the Eastern wing to go its own way so that he could become the president of what was left of Pakistan. Bhutto came straight to the point. He wanted me to agree that the three areas – Foreign Affairs, Defence and Communications – would be managed jointly by Pakistan and Bangladesh. I told him it was not possible but then he went on pressing for it until I said that it was difficult for me to decide anything without consulting my people. There was yet another meeting, the last one between us. That time too, he pressed for the same thing and asked me to do my best. I replied: 'Let me see.'

When I told Mujib what Bhutto had said, particularly his assertion that Mujib had sworn by the Koran to allow joint control of some subjects, Mujib said: 'Bhutto is a liar. I am grateful to him for saving my life, but that gives him no right to spread lies.'

The versions were as different as the personalities of the two. Bhutto was flamboyant, dapper and uncertain; Mujib was retiring, simple and forthright. The former blew hot and cold in the same breath; the latter showed trust and steadfastness. At least one thing emerged from the talks between the two. Mujib was released unconditionally on 8 January, 1972. He was requested to go to any Arab country and then fly to Dhaka or Delhi or wherever he pleased. But he preferred to go to London before he returned to Dhaka via New Delhi.

After the meeting between Mujib and Bhutto, the follow-up dialogue was reported to have been carried out between Bhutto and Kamal Hasan, later the foreign minister in Bangladesh. He was also released from a West Pakistani jail after Mujib was set free. Islamabad reported that Kamal was supposed to have carried a message for Mujib on links between Pakistan and Bangladesh. But when I met him in Dhaka Mujib said this was not true.

Bhutto's purpose in releasing Mujib – 'a nightingale whom I allowed to go scot-free, unnecessarily' – as Bhutto described him to me, was to retrieve, in the eyes of the international community, at least something of Pakistan's image which had been shattered by the Islamabad Army's killing of hundreds of intellectuals before the surrender. Bhutto told me three months later that he had released Mujib as a gesture to India, whom he knew would find the going hard in Bangladesh without Mujib. Mujib's release did not mean any change in Pakistan policy on Bangladesh. Islamabad carried on as if there was no war or no liberation of Bangladesh. Bhutto spoke Yahya Khan's language. In his first broadcast as president (20 December, 1971), he said: 'We will continue to fight for the honour and integrity of Pakistan. East Pakistan is an inseparable and unseverable part of Pakistan.'

Radio Pakistan also did its bit to keep up the fiction, by continuing to begin its daily transmission with the announcement of the time not only in West Pakistan but also in 'East Pakistan'. West Pakistani newspapers, which used to have editions published from Dhaka, continued to claim simultaneous publication in 'East Pakistan' on their mastheads. Whenever Rawalpindi talked of convening the Pakistan National Assembly, it took pains to mention 'the representatives of East Pakistan' among the members to attend. Pakistan changed only after the Shimla Conference between Indira Gandhi and Bhutto.

32

The Shimla Agreement

AFTER MY RETURN FROM PAKISTAN, THE FIRST TWO VIPS WHO asked me to meet them, were the then petroleum minister D.P. Dhar, and the then prime minister Indira Gandhi in that order. In my absence, Dhar had been nominated India's special envoy to Islamabad to work out an agenda for a conference between Mrs Gandhi and Pakistan president, Zulfikar Ali Bhutto. Shimla was the venue selected by her for its cool climate and historical importance. Since I was the first Indian journalist to have met Bhutto after the Bangladesh War, the government was keen to understand his thought process and sought my assessment.

I spent two-and-a-half hours with Dhar in the presence of Ashok Chib, then the joint secretary looking after Pakistan. Dhar was kind enough to remark after the meeting that he was able to get a real feel of Pakistan and the problems it was facing after his discussion with me. One point that he checked with me again and again was the observation made by Bhutto during the interview to me that the ceasefire line was the 'the line of peace'. I played back the tape-recorder to satisfy him. The line of peace idea was pursued by Mrs Gandhi with Bhutto at Shimla in 1972. He reportedly told her not to insist on it because he would run into difficulties in his own country.

My meeting with Mrs Gandhi lasted for half an hour and I gave her the gist of what Bhutto had said. As we were getting up, she asked me which option India should exercise between returning occupied territory and Pakistani prisoners of war. I told her that, left to me, I would have returned prisoners and the occupied territory after the fall of Dhaka. The Pakistani people would have taken their soldiers to task for the defeat. On the other hand, the longer they stayed in India as prisoners of the enemy, the higher their stock would be in Pakistan when they returned home after having undergone imprisonment.

Indeed, when we released the prisoners months later, they were received like heroes. Similarly, had we returned the territory soon after Pakistan's defeat, this voluntary act of generosity would have boosted our prestige.

Bhutto had told me that India would not be able to keep the prisoners of war for long because of the pressure of world opinion. He had already started sending postcards on behalf of the POWs' children, saying that India was keeping their fathers in custody. It touched a chord of sympathy. Mrs Gandhi said she was helpless because the prisoners had surrendered before the joint command of India and Bangladesh; Sheikh Mujib-ur-Rehman, the president of Bangladesh, she said, was not yet willing to release them.

Bhutto's first priority was the vacating of territory. Being a Sindhi, he was under pressure in his home state on this point because two-thirds of the territory occupied by India was in Sind and Kutch, totalling 4,765.17 square miles. About a million people belonging to the Shakargarh area had taken shelter in and around Sialkot. He would have been in a more chastened mood, ready to talk about peace in the subcontinent, if India had used occupied territory as a bargaining point. Bhutto brought his daughter Benazir with him to Shimla and she became the focus of the media's attention.

Also accompanying Bhutto was Mazar Ali Khan, Tariq Ali's father. Mazar knew Mrs Gandhi's secretary P.N. Haksar very well. Both belonged to the left. Mazar played an important role behind the scenes.

The Government of India had arranged to bug Bhutto's living quarters, including the bathroom. It was clear on the very first day that Bhutto was not willing to convert the ceasefire line into the international border between India and Pakistan. Subsequently, he said that he was agreeable but he would not give this in writing because he had yet to prepare his country for it. This was not true.

The moment he returned to Lahore he told his close friends in the Pakistan People's Party to denounce the Shimla Agreement. Having made several visits to Pakistan after the Shimla Agreement, I was convinced that Bhutto, even if he was sincere, could not have sold the idea of recognizing the ceasefire line as the international border to his fellow Pakistanis at that time. The defeat in Bangladesh had hardened public opinion, more so that of the armed forces. If he had conceded on the ceasefire line, Bhutto would have been thrown out by them much earlier than he eventually was.

The substitution of Dhar by Haksar as the Indian delegation's leader was inevitable. Dhar and state foreign minister, Aziz Ahmed, leader of Pakistan's delegation, were covering the same ground that they had done when they had met at Murree, only a month earlier, to prepare the ground for the summit. Dhar kept emphasizing the need for a durable settlement, including Kashmir, and Aziz his priorities of releasing the POWs and vacating territory. Finally, Dhar feigned a heart problem and Haksar stepped in. He used all his persuasive power to make Aziz agree that the solution to the Kashmir problem lay in recognizing the ceasefire line as the international border.

As a compromise of sorts, Bhutto agreed to convert the ceasefire line into the Line of Control (LoC). But he made it clear that he was not willing to accept the ceasefire line as the international border. Mrs Gandhi intervened to argue that Kashmir could be solved once and for all by converting the ceasefire line into the international border. Bhutto pleaded with her to keep Kashmir out because then the whole Agreement would become suspect in the eyes of the Pakistanis.

'My back is to the wall; I cannot make any more concessions,' said Bhutto. He suggested that the decision on Kashmir be postponed to some other time. 'Why hurry on these matters? I think haste sometimes ruins these problems. And why should it be incumbent on us to solve all problems?' he said. He repeated that he would not to be able to 'sell' any formula on Kashmir to his country at the present time.

Eventually, the talks broke down because New Delhi wanted some 'commitment' on Kashmir before releasing the POWs or vacating the territory. Mazhar met Mrs Gandhi and warned her that the failure of the Shimla Summit would mean the beginning of Bhutto's downfall and the ultimate return of the army. She relented. Bhutto agreed to respect 'the line of control resulting from the ceasefire of 17 December, 1971'. But after this sentence, he added in his own hand in the Draft Agreement, 'without prejudice to the recognized position of either side'. India agreed to this.

The Agreement was signed at 12.40 a.m. on 3 July 1972 – after almost everyone had decided that the summit had failed.

So late and unexpected was this development that no typewriter was at hand to prepare a corrected copy of the Agreement, nor was the Pakistan Government's seal available, since it had already been packed in a box and sent by road to Chandigarh with other pieces of heavy baggage which could not have been taken by helicopter from Shimla. As the Pakistan seal could not be put on the document, India also did not put its seal on it.

Still, the Shimla Agreement was an official document. The Agreement was only one small step in a long journey. For India, it was an exercise in good faith; a symbol of trust, which it expected, would beget trust. Except for the Jana Sangh and the Socialist Party, practically all the other political parties welcomed the Agreement. In Pakistan, the opposition came only from Muslim diehards. People on both sides were relieved because they saw in the Agreement a silver lining in the dark cloud of suspicion and distrust which had hung over the subcontinent for twenty-five years.

But whether the lining would lengthen or the cloud would expand was difficult to foretell at that time. Much depended on the prospects of a Kashmir settlement. For Indians, the state was an integral part of their country; for the Pakistanis it was a territory which belonged to them, or should belong to them. It was impossible to reconcile both these viewpoints. But perhaps the two sides could agree to a cooling off. They could, for instance agree to create a 'soft' border along the ceasefire line, pending a permanent solution or the 'hardening' of the status quo.

33

A Prime Minister Is Assassinated

YAHYA BAKHTIAR, ZULFIKAR ALI BHUTTO'S LAWYER, WAS ONE
year senior to me at Law College in Lahore. I had barely
checked into Flashman's Hotel in Rawalpindi in 1979 when
he sent me a message asking for a meeting. He had learnt of
my presence in the city because a local Urdu newspaper
carried a news report about my visit to Pakistan.

Yahya's home was within walking distance from my hotel.
When I met him, he came to the point straightaway. Bhutto's
mercy petition was pending before General Zia-ul-Haq,
Pakistan's martial law administrator. Bhutto, Yahya said, had
read about my visit and had asked him (his lawyer) if I could
find out more about the outcome of his mercy petition during
my forthcoming interview with Zia. I promised Yahya to do
my best.

I had great regard for Bhutto. He was one person in
Pakistan who talked in terms of economic programmes instead
of the usual religious mumbo jumbo which I heard all over
the country. For a journalist, he was good copy because he
would always respond with a quotable quote.

He was vain, without any doubt, and seemed to genuinely
believe in his intellectual superiority to all others. He once

told me that if merit was the criterion, he deserved to be the prime minister of the subcontinent. Mrs Indira Gandhi was then India's prime minister and Sheikh Mujib-ur-Rehman the Bangladesh president. Bhutto would compare himself with Jawaharlal Nehru. Yet, for all his popular rhetoric, Bhutto was an authoritarian at heart. He did not like critics and went to any lengths to silence them.

I didn't have to wait long for an interview with Zia because he liked talking to me and found in me a good listener. He once told me the whole story of his military takeover, stretching over an hour, and I was all ears. I wrote a piece about it, without making any value judgement, which I was told pleased him. He was also happy that he could switch to Punjabi, Urdu or English whenever he felt like during his conversation with me. Strangely, he was particular in making sure that every interview was recorded.

Discussing Indo–Pakistan relations was not difficult. But my mission was different. I had to find out whether he was going to hang Bhutto and if so, when. I recalled how Zia had told me once that when he met Bhutto at Murree after the coup, the latter had tried to placate him by remarking that 'with your brawn and my brain, we can rule Pakistan forever'. He said that Bhutto had pleaded with him in that vein for a long time. Here was my chance, I thought.

I asked him what formalities needed to be observed to dispose of a mercy petition. I deliberately held back from mentioning Bhutto. He said that there was no mystery involved, merely routine contact with the authorities concerned to confirm whether the sentenced person was indeed guilty of committing the crime for which the punishment was death by hanging. He also explained that the entire procedure could be expedited over the telephone. From this I inferred that a decision on Bhutto's fate would be taken sooner rather than later. Knowing well that he was the final authority, I asked Zia who would ultimately take the decision; he replied that he would.

At this juncture, I introduced Bhutto's name. I told him that some reports indicated there was great pressure on him to commute Bhutto's death sentence to life imprisonment. He took no time to reply: 'No pressure,' he said candidly. I told him I had heard that both Saudi Arabia and the US had requested him not to hang Bhutto. This time Zia didn't reply directly and merely repeated that there was no pressure on him from any quarter. People believed, Zia said, that it was either Bhutto's neck or his own. The court had given its decision. He had nothing more to say.

I once again brought the discussion back to Bhutto's petition. I imagined, I told him, that it would take him another month to complete the process, as it was a large exercise. He interrupted me to enquire when I was going back. Tomorrow, I replied. He was surprised, as if my reply had jolted him. 'Oh,' he said loudly. I thought the way he reacted was significant. I changed the subject and reminded him of his promise to hold elections within ninety days. His reply was cursory and casual.

That evening, I told Yahya that I believed that Bhutto would be hanged and that it would be soon, in the next few days. The following afternoon, before leaving Rawalpindi, I went to say goodbye to Yahya Khan. By then he had met Bhutto. He told me that when he conveyed my assessment to Bhutto, the latter replied that Kuldip had got it wrong because there was a lot of pressure on Zia not to hang him.

~

Within two days of my return to Delhi, on 4 April 1979, I heard that Bhutto had been hanged. Islamabad preferred a foreign agency, the BBC, to the media in Pakistan and India to announce his death. The news made me sad. Bhutto was one of the most intelligent men I had known in the subcontinent. Moreover, the elimination of an opponent by hanging was a first in Pakistan's history.

Yahya must have realized that my assessment had been correct. I wish I had been wrong. The elimination of a democratically elected prime minister by a tinpot military dictator was not good for any country. In fact, before the hanging I had met the main opposition leaders, Wali Khan from the NWFP and Asghar Khan from Punjab – to request them to issue a statement to support Bhutto's mercy petition but both of them spurned my plea. They said that only the military could save Bhutto who, both agreed, was determined to wipe out their political opponents. Wali talked about the attempt on his own life that Bhutto had supposedly approved.

Whatever a popular leader's limitations, he had to be dealt with democratically since he was an elected leader. The voters in India did this when they defeated Mrs Indira Gandhi and her Congress party after the excesses they committed during the Emergency.

I was disappointed when I saw no popular reaction in Pakistan to Bhutto's death. People were afraid to open their mouths. Ironically, there were demonstrations across the border, in India, lamenting his fate. The Indian media also showed its unhappiness. Bhutto's loss was bemoaned in editorials and on special programmes on T.V. The government, under Morarji Desai, was careful not to say anything. However, one slogan in India that gained popular currency in those days was: 'Bhutto Hum Sharminda Hain. Terey Katil Zinda Hain! (Bhutto, we are ashamed that your killers are alive).

Some years later, one of the judges, a Parsi gentleman, who was part of the Bench that confirmed the death sentence on Bhutto, came to Delhi. We met at a dinner.

He told me he had registered my presence in the court during the hearings. But he blamed Bhutto's lawyer, Yahya Bakhtiar for the tragic outcome. His argument was that Yahya stretched the case unnecessarily. At one stage, he said, the majority of judges were on Bhutto's side. Then one judge retired and was replaced by another who was Zia's man. Those in favour of Bhutto, who were keen to set him free, lost the majority overnight. The Parsi judge said that he had hinted to Yahya many a time to wind up his argument quickly but failed to make him see the point. Since I never met Yahya again, I could not ask him whether in fact he had unnecessarily prolonged the case.

Once, on another trip to Pakistan, a tall man came up to me at an evening party in Islamabad. He took me aside and said that he was one of the judges who had concurred with the dissenting verdict. Although now retired, he was being harassed by Zia's intelligence agencies. He also spoke of his fear that he might be killed. He wanted my help to escape from Pakistan. I told him that the India–Pakistan border was too heavily guarded to be a viable option. I suggested that the best way was to slip into Afghanistan from the NWFP open borders. Subsequently, I learnt that he had taken my advice and reached London via Kabul. By the time I tried to contact him in London, he had died. I would have liked him to tell me why he had voted for Bhutto's exoneration despite being one of Bhutto's victims. Apparently, long before the military coup, Bhutto had personally intervened to ensure that he was superceded by another judge in Lahore's High Court.

34

Jayawardene and the Tamil Tigers

I STAYED WITH THE INDIAN HIGH COMMISSIONER J.N. DIXIT IN Colombo when I interviewed President Junius Jayawardene in 1985. Dixit had nobody else living with him in his house – a huge, double-storeyed structure. He was operating from there because India was considered an enemy country by the Sinhalese. Only a week earlier, some extremists among them had burnt down Indian shops and houses in the capital to vent their anger against New Delhi. The general belief was that India was assisting the 'hostile Tamils' in the north who were out to carve a separate country, Eelam, from Sri Lanka.

This was not entirely true because though we armed and trained the Eelam supporters, New Delhi was not so foolish as to establish an independent Tamil state in Sri Lanka when the embers for the demand for a sovereign Tamil Nadu in Indian were still smouldering even after more than a decade. The then Tamil Nadu chief minister M. Karunanidhi was in constant touch with the Tamil Eelam proponents, but only to keep them on his side. He had informed New Delhi that his interest lay in getting a better deal for the Tamils in Sri Lanka, lest India be swamped by refugees seeking shelter from the Sinhalese bias.

What I saw in Colombo left me in no doubt that the burning or demolition of Indian shops and houses had been done meticulously with the connivance of the authorities. In a row of Sinhalese properties, only the Indian shops had been targeted for destruction. I had seen the same pattern during communal riots in India, where Muslim and Sikh establishments were destroyed but not the ones belonging to the Hindus next door.

The Indians in Colombo were fairly well off. Dixit agreed with me that the Sinhalese were upset with India but it was a phenomenon which would not last long. He believed that they had no recourse but to face the fact of India's 'size and might'. Dixit was like a hawk. I had watched him working, first in Dhaka and later in Islamabad. But it must be said to his credit that he was keen to have good relations with the neighbouring countries; although on India's terms. He had a similar attitude towards Sri Lanka. I could also discern in him a soft spot for the Liberation Tigers of Tamil Eelam (LTTE). But it was only to the extent of an articulation of the Tamils' share in the affairs of Sri Lanka. He was firmly opposed to the LTTE's stand for a separate homeland, realizing its repercussions on India. He, however, favoured autonomy for the 'north' within Sri Lanka. Dixit was keen to know what Jayawardene would say in the interview to me because there was practically no diplomatic contact between New Delhi and Colombo.

Sri Lanka was indignant with India because of the training and arms it had given the LTTE. Dixit was not unnecessarily worried over this point. His unhappiness was that India's involvement had leaked out. To me, India's role betrayed duplicity. On the one hand, we avowed friendship to the Sri Lankan government and on the other we gave training and weapons to the LTTE.

This was precisely the sentiment Jayawardene conveyed to me when he suddenly summoned me. 'Prime Minister Rajiv Gandhi is the captain of the South Asian ship,' he said.

'Wherever he takes us will be the destination. It all depends on him, India, and you. The question that bothers me is, are you taking the right course?'

Jayawardene was buoyant and confident, in sharp contrast to the diffident and worried figure he had cut when I had last interviewed him one year ago. Asked what had happened between then and now to change his tone and tenor, he beamed: 'I am winning the war.' Subsequently, he said: 'I find Prime Minister Rajiv Gandhi more accommodating than his mother, Mrs Indira Gandhi. He must do in Sri Lanka what he did in Punjab and Assam. As I said at the SAARC meeting, he cannot fail us.'

'Why do you doubt India?' I asked him.

'Because you have trained the LTTE. You still give them arms. What can I do when you give them shelter after they have killed my people and destroyed our property? You can take stern action against the LTTE by cutting off aid. But it is strange that you should continue to help them even when they are out to break up my country.'

Jayawardene sounded bitter and threatened to seek help from Pakistan, China or America to thwart what he described as 'India's double-faced policy' to run with the hare and hunt with the hounds. After giving me a bit of his mind, he relaxed and resumed smoking his cigar ('They are from Cuba. Fidel Castro sends me the consignment regularly'). 'I shall have a military solution to what I believe is a military problem. After doing so, I shall tackle the political side,' he said.

I knew he was annoyed with India but still depended on it to improve relations with the Tamils in the north. I was anxious to know how far he was willing to accommodate the Tamils; possibly giving provincial autonomy to the areas where the LTTE was strong. New Delhi had suggested this to him. But he never came to accept the suggestion because he was sold on a unitary form of government and did not want even a wisp of a federal structure. He believed in force and felt that, if India were to stay away, he could succeed militarily and crush the LTTE's 'insurgency'. Whenever he mentioned a solution, he only talked in terms of military action and 'foreign assistance'. He made no secret of the fact that he was training a large contingent in Pakistan and Israel.

Jayawardene's child-like belief was that, once he had trained his army, he would be able to eliminate the Eelam. Yet he was willing to come to a settlement because he knew that India would not leave the Eelam supporters in the lurch.

What surprised me was when Jayawardene said that he was all for devolving power to the Tamils. But there were many ifs and buts. The Tamils could not have any share in the law and order machinery.

All this time, Jayawardene questioned me about New Delhi's attitude. He was pleased by Rajiv Gandhi's gesture of removing a rigid G. Parthasarathi from the talks and putting Foreign Secretary Romesh Bhandari in his place. (Jayawardene had earlier expressed distrust in GP – who had put pressure on Rajiv Gandhi not to remove him because he had the confidence of the Tamil leaders in India.)

On my return, I reported the gist of my interview with Jayawardene to Dixit. I never understood what was so urgent or so important in the interview that sent Dixit scurrying to send a message to Rajiv Gandhi. New Delhi already knew that Jayawardene was training his troops in Pakistan and Israel so that couldn't be the reason for Dixit's SOS. Perhaps, Jayawardene's observation that Rajiv Gandhi could lead the region struck Dixit as favourable and he saw it as a starting point for talks with Jayawardene.

Following the publication of my interview with Jayawardene, there was optimism in India. New Delhi intensified its efforts to span the distance between the LTTE and the Sri Lankan government. Ultimately, Colombo was able to persuade New Delhi to send in its forces, the Indian Peace Keeping Force (IPKF).

The IPKF was a failure. Dixit had misread the Sri Lankan message. However, it made India wiser. It decided then not to get involved any further in the affairs of Sri Lanka – a decision it has stood by till this day.

35

Bus Diplomacy

ON 20 FEBRUARY 1999, I WAS SITTING BEHIND PRIME MINISTER
Atal Behari Vajpayee on the bus going to Lahore, at the
invitation of Pakistan's prime minister, Nawaz Sharif. En
route, before reaching the Wagah border, Vajpayee beckoned
to me and informed me that he had received news about the
killing of some 26 Hindus by militants in the Jammu division.
He was anguished by the latest killings and wondered whether
there was any use in further talks. I tried to reassure him by
saying that the militants were so desperate to stall the talks
with Nawaz Sharif that they were killing only to provoke the
Hindus. He saw my point but was not sure how Indian opinion
would react to his visiting Pakistan despite the killings.

A worried Vajpayee entered Pakistan amid festivities on
both sides of the border. The welcome ceremony was short
and simple. The three service chiefs of Pakistan were present
but did not salute Vajpayee. Vajpayee flew with Nawaz Sharif
to Lahore in a helicopter while we travelled on in the same
bus.

The drive reminded me of the Partition – of the time
when I had walked from my hometown, Sialkot city, to Lahore.
Now I was in a vehicle covering the same road between

Amritsar and Lahore. But this time there were no dead bodies, burnt vehicles or scattered luggage. Men and women, standing in their fields or beside their houses, waved to us vigorously. We waved back. There was hardly any difference between this countryside and the one which we had left behind in India.

In Lahore, we were put up in a 5-star hotel. After changing hurriedly, we reached the governor's house where Vajpayee was staying, to accompany him to the banquet at the Qila (Fort). It was a long wait of more than two hours and nobody told us the reason for the delay. Ultimately, Vajpayee, along with his secretary and others, emerged from the building. Only then did we learn that the road to the Fort had been, quite literally, taken over by the Jamaat-e-Islami. Its members and supporters had turned back all vehicles and had even stoned some diplomats' cars.

As we drove down the road to the Fort we could see piles of bricks stacked on both sides. Shabaz Sharif, chief minister of Pakistan's Punjab, told me that the Jamaat had promised to protest only for a few minutes but it had played false. I imagined that an agreement had probably been the only way out because the Jamaat had a strong presence in Lahore.

Vajpayee read out his banquet speech in English. It was flat. Apparently, it had been pieced together by some bureaucrats. These were the same bureaucrats who had at one time decided that the leaders of different political parties would accompany Vajpayee to Lahore. When I learned about this, I had prevailed upon Vajpayee's principal secretary, Brajesh Mishra, and convinced him that the prime minister would be more appreciated if he were accompanied by eminent artists, writers and scientists; this way Pakistan would get the message that Vajpayee had the backing of the intelligentsia.

Vajpayee's speech was as much a disaster as a delegation of politicians would have been. Even if there was a message, it was lost in the involved sentences and familiar clichés. The only relief was provided by the profusely decorated Fort and the shaded lights silhouetting the large trees and lighting up the grassy grounds.

The following morning, I met Vajpayee and told him that his speech at the civic reception later in the day should be in his own words, drawn both from Urdu and Hindi. He agreed, and his words went down so well that even today people recall his speech with nostalgia. He told the audience that Pakistan did not need anyone's recognition because it had its own identity and recognition. Earlier, he had written in the visitors' book at Minar-e-Pakistan, (where the Pakistan Resolution was passed) that the integrity and prosperity of India depended upon the integrity and prosperity of Pakistan.

While the two prime ministers were busy talking, the rest of the delegation was attending a lunch hosted by Sahebzada Yakub Khan, once Pakistan's foreign minister. Both of us sat at the same table. The conversation was very informative. He asked the person sitting next to me to which place he belonged. He replied that he was from the North-West Frontier Province. Sahebzada's next question was: How did he see Kashmir? He replied: 'A distant land which does not interest me in one way or the other.' A similar response came from two other persons sitting at the table. One of them was from Sind and the other from Baluchistan. Sahibzada then turned towards me and said: 'This was your problem; of the Punjabis on both sides. You should settle it.'

A friend of mine, Mushahid Hussain, former information minister in the Nawaz Sharif Cabinet, was Vajpayee's minister-in-waiting. He told me later that the Lahore Declaration which Nawaz Sharif and Vajpayee had signed was the best thing that could happen to the two countries. There was also a road map for the settlement of Kashmir as well as a time frame. He did not give me any details, although he, a hardliner, was positive about the Declaration.

Little did I know at that time that the Kargil operation had almost started. Nawaz Sharif – whom I checked with in Jeddah where he was living after General Pervez Musharraf had banished him after the coup – said that he did not know anything about Kargil until Vajpayee informed him about the intrusion on the hotline. However, General Pervez Musharraf said in a later interview that 'everybody was on board'.

I suspect Nawaz Sharif had some prior information about the operation, in much the same way that General Ayub Khan knew about the infiltration which Zulfikar Ali Bhutto had arranged in 1965, leading to a war between India and Pakistan.

At our meeting in Jeddah, Nawaz Sharif told me that he had paid the price for trying to negotiate peace with India; an issue to which, he said, the military had been opposed. This might well be true. For any kind of settlement on Kashmir, the Pakistanis say without hesitation that the military would have to be involved; they would not agree to any arrangement which meant the transfer of power from it to the civil.

When I met Vajpayee after the coup in Pakistan, he said 'He (Nawaz Sharif) sacrificed himself for us.' Regarding the settlement on Kashmir, Vajpayee said, 'We were almost there.' He was referring to the behind-the-scene talks between former newspaperman R.K. Mishra and Niaz Naik, the former foreign secretary of Pakistan. I failed to scoop on what the agreement was which made Vajpayee say, 'We were almost there.'

R.K. Mishra has not opened his mouth. Niaz Naik has said in subsequent press interviews that the settlement still had a lot to cover. So, exactly what direction the talk between Mishra and Niaz took, for Vajpayee to remark 'we were almost there', is not known yet.